Chester Allen Winton, Associate Professor of Sociology and Associate Dean of Graduate Studies at San Jose State University, received his Ph.D. from the University of California at Berkeley in 1970. Professor Winton has conducted research on blindness as a fellow of the National Institute of Mental Health and Vocational Rehabilitation Administration. Several articles resulting from this research have been published in professional journals and in *Science and Progress: Retrospective and Prospective.* In addition to his academic and research duties, Professor Winton is licensed by the state of California as a Family, Marriage and Child counselor.

THEORY AND MEASUREMENT IN SOCIOLOGY

by Chester A. Winton

A Halsted Press Book

SCHENKMAN PUBLISHING COMPANY

John Wiley & Sons, Inc

New York, London, Sydney, Toronto

Library of Congress Cataloging in Publication Data

Winton, Chester A
    Theory and measurement in sociology.

    "A Halsted Press book."
       1. Sociology--Methodology.   2. Sociology--Statistical methods.   3. Sociological research.   I. Title.
    HM24.W55   301'.01'8   74-9539
    ISBN 0-470-95515-5

Copyright © 1974
Schenkman Publishing Company, Inc.
Cambridge, Massachusetts

Distributed solely by Halsted Press, a division
of John Wiley & Sons, Inc. New York

Library of Congress Catalog Card Number: 73-84745
Printed in the United States of America

All rights reserved. This book or parts thereof,
may not be reproduced in any form without
written permission of the publisher.
A Halsted Press Book

To Susie, Michelle and Jeffrey,
who waited patiently

ACKNOWLEDGMENTS

I wish to thank Winfield W. Salisbury and Roy G. Francis for reading and improving drafts of this book. I wish to thank Harold Hodges and Charles Mohler for the confidence they showed in me. And I thank my family, particularly Susan and Michelle, who with great patience and understanding, made many sacrifices.

CONTENTS

Introduction   1

Chapter 1: Measurement and Theory   4

Chapter 2: Measurement and Theory Creation   27

Chapter 3: Evaluating Sociological Theory   66

COPYRIGHT ACKNOWLEDGMENTS

Grateful acknowledgment is made to the following for permission to use materials herein.

The Literary Executor of the late Sir Ronald A. Fisher, F.R.S., and to Oliver and Boyd, Edinburgh, for permission to reprint the Chi Square table from their book *Statistical Tables for Biological, Agricultural, and Medical Research.*

The University of Chicago Press for permission to use a table of occupational rankings from an article by Hodge, Seigel and Rossi, "Occupational Prestige in the United States," *American Journal of Sociology*, 1964.

Prentice-Hall, Inc. for permission to use material from James A. Davis, *Elementary Survey Analysis* (Englewood Cliffs: Prentice-Hall, 1971).

McGraw-Hill Book Company for permission to use population pyramids from Thompson and Lewis, *Population Problems*, 5th Edition, Copyright 1965.

Harper & Row Publishers, Inc. for permission to quote from Roger Barker and Herbert F. Wright's book, *One Boy's Day* (New York: Harper & Row, 1951).

INTRODUCTION

In 1962, my first year of graduate school at the University of California in Berkeley, I was asked to read some essays in Robert Merton's book *Social Theory and Social Structure*. In two of those essays, Merton formulates what appeared to me at the time to be a very logical, almost simplistic argument; namely, that empirical research and sociological theory exist in a symbiotic relationship. Each has no meaning, no significance without the other. They cannot be separated inasmuch as they are integral parts of a singular sociological enterprise—the building of a body of knowledge about human group life.

In one essay, Merton views "The Bearing of Empirical Research on Sociological Theory" as follows:

> It is my central thesis that empirical research goes far beyond the passive role of verifying and testing theory: it does more than confirm or refute hypotheses. Research plays an active role: it performs at least four major functions which help shape the development of theory. It initiates, it reformulates, it deflects and it clarifies theory.[1]

Merton published this in 1949. Although these essays were widely read and widely quoted in the 1950's and 1960's, the thoughts contained in these essays seem to have had little impact on the structure of American sociology. Sociologists still tend to identify themselves as being theorists *or* methodologists. College and university curricula usually offer separate couses in sociological theory or sociological research; it is rare to find a course on the interrelation of theory and research or on the sociological process from a holistic perspective. Given this state of affairs, it seems timely to write this book as a reiteration and explication of what Merton told us two decades ago.

I am reminded of an acquaintance who is a gestalt therapist. As we talked on a beautiful, quiet day in a thick redwood forest, he told me of

---

[1] Robert K. Merton, "The Bearing of Empirical Research on Sociological Theory" in Robert K. Merton, *On Theoretical Sociology* (New York: Free Press, 1967) p. 157; and in Robert K. Merton, *Social Theory and Social Structure* (New York: Free Press of Glencoe, 1957) p. 103.

work he was doing with young boys who had difficulty catching baseballs. Physiological tests indicated that there was no reason why these boys should not be able to catch a ball. They had normal sight, normal co-ordination, and normal reflexes. Ruling out physiological causes of their difficulty, my friend sought psychological causes. He hypothesized that, as a result of past difficulties encountered in catching baseballs, they had acquired a little voice within them that said, as the ball sailed in their direction, "You know you're not going to catch that ball!" Sure enough, that voice expressed a self-fulfilling prophecy. The boy does not catch the ball because the voice distracts him, it breaks his concentration on the ball.

All of us have voices within us, telling us that we cannot do things. Maybe the voice tells us we cannot fix the car or the television set, maybe it tells us we cannot do the algebra or statistics problem, maybe it tells us we cannot write or understand poetry. The voice within distracts us, prevents us from concentrating on the problem at hand, and, sure enough, we don't complete it successfully.

Professional sociologists and sociology students have voices within them also. The "voices", as we have called them, are really the individual telling himself that he can understand theory but just can't grasp statistics or social research, or that he can understand the statistics and research but can't dig the theory. So he concentrates on what he thinks he can do and ignores, as much as possible, what his voice tells him he cannot do.

By ignoring either theory or measurement, the individual becomes a pseudo-sociologist. He loses perspective on the total sociological process, and in so doing, loses the rationale for what he is doing, whether that be theory building or empirical research.

It is my contention that one of the reasons sociology students are turned off to statistics and research is that they fail to see its function in the total sociological enterprise. Taught as an isolated subject, research easily loses its relevance. It becomes an intellectual exercise, leading students to ask "so what?"

Theory, when it is isolated, becomes difficult to understand, for without linking it to research, one cannot comprehend how it is created nor how it is evaluated and continuously changed. It is from the perspective of the methodologist that one realizes that theory is not static, but forever subject to change.

In this book, my purpose is to show how theory and measurement in sociology are intertwined. It is my hope that when sociology is seen in a total perspective, students will come to understand why they must learn the dynamics of both theory building and research. It is my further hope that this introduction will give students some insight into the fact that the enemy in understanding sociology is not the subject matter, but the student himself, with all his voices which tell him what he cannot comprehend. If your hang-up is sociological theory, this book will help you to view theory from a perspective with which you are comfortable, for theory is the product of research and is evaluated and changed by research. If your hang-up is research and statistics, you should find it helpful to examine research and statistics as parts of theory-building, for theory comes out of research and is refined by it. If you are hung-up on both sociological theory and social research and statistics, then this book will be rough going.

The first chapter of this book places measurement within a theoretical context. It illustrates how measurement and theory are part of a single sociological process. It attempts to demonstrate the relevance of measurement to theoretical sociology.

The second chapter examines how theory is created through social research. Two research designs frequently used by sociologists are "survey research" and "field work." Two sociological theories are created using each of these designs.

The third chapter of the book explores how theory is evaluated and changed through measurement. The ultimate worth of any theory is based upon whether it enables us to predict and understand events in the real world. We evaluate theories by applying them to reality and seeing if they fit, if they are accurate. Where they are not accurate enough, we must alter them.

The book ends with a reiteration of its basic thesis. Measurement is an integral part of both theory-building and social research. The measurements made in research come out of theory and in turn are used to evaluate theory. In the process, they may create new theory. Measurement links theory and research on human group life into the single unified process we call sociology.

CHAPTER 1

MEASUREMENT AND THEORY

Sociologists usually focus on the systematic character of social life. They perceive human group life as constituting a system. A system is a boundary maintained entity which is composed of interrelated and interdependent parts. When the sociologist examines social settings, small groups, organizations, communities or societies as systems, he describes the component parts of the systems and then analyzes how these parts are interrelated and interdependent. The sociologist calls this a description of the *social structure* of a system.

We are going to view sociology as a system. Theory and research are parts of this system. They are, further, systems themselves, sub-systems of sociology. In this chapter, we will examine how they are interrelated and interdependent.

One goal of sociology is to create a body of theory which will describe and account for regularities of human behavior. From where does this theory come? Theories come from measurements of the real world, whether those measurements be formal and systematic or not. Theories are the articulated observations of men who detect regularities in human group life. The perception of these regularities involves objective or subjective measurement, inasmuch as regularities are seen as occurring with some degree of frequency, relative to other behavior which is seen as being more random. Theories are born out of a man's observation of statistical regularity. Theories come from measurement and research.

Once they exist, they are tested and evaluated by means of measurement and research. Theories are only useful if they accurately describe and predict human behavior. They must continuously be tested and evaluated to assess the degree to which they are accurate and thus useful.

When one does social research, the kinds of measurements taken always have some theoretical relevance. How does one know what is important to measure and what is not important to measure? How does one know who should and who should not be included as respondents in a study? How does one know how to analyze data once it is collected? The answers to these questions are given in the structure of the theory one is evaluating. The logic and strategy of social research has a theoretical base. Research is only meaningful in a theoretical context; one comes to understand why research takes the form that it does rather than some other form only when conceptual definitions and hypotheses, which are parts of theories, are taken into account.

THE COMPONENTS OF THEORY

We have been discussing the term "theory" rather loosely. To fully understand how theory and measurement are linked, it is important to know what theory is. The word theory is used in many different ways by sociologists. It is sometimes used to refer to a theoretical model, a way of perceiving reality, which imposes a perceptual framework or structure on that reality. This is a kind of social philosophy which is sometimes labeled "theory". Social evolutionary theory, structural-functional theory, symbolic interaction theory are examples of such theoretical models which are used by sociologists.

But this is not the kind of theory we will be discussing in this book. The kind of theory we will discuss is called axiomatic theory. *Sociological axiomatic theory consists of logically related, logically consistent, and logically complete definitions and propositions about human group life.* In analyzing the structure of axiomatic theory, we will examine the component parts of such theories and then show how these parts are interrelated. It is only when we understand what theory is that we can comprehend how theory and measurement are linked.

TERMS: Theories are made of words or terms. Terms which are common to sociology include "norms", "values", "society", "social class", "social role", "mores", "folkways", and so forth. Terms are words used to label or signify some concept or idea.

CONCEPTS: A concept is a mental abstraction, an idea, in the mind of a man. Though "norms", "values", "society", "social class", and "social role" are words, they also signify an idea, a conceptualization of what that word means. What "society" means to a sociologist, the mental image which is evoked by this word, is the sociologist's concept of society. The term "society" is only a label for the mental image of what societies are. We could call the concept anything we chose; terms are arbitrary. The mental abstraction itself, however, has meaning.

Concepts enable man to categorize, interpret, structure, and thus make some sense of the world. The everyday man on the street structures his world with concepts of trees, birds, occupations, sex, money and so forth. The concepts we employ in everyday life to structure and categorize the world are part of what we call "culture".

The sociologist structures his world with concepts which differ from those of the man on the street. Usually the sociologist cannot use the concepts of everyday life because these concepts are too vague for his needs. The goals of the sociologist and the man on the street are different. The man on the street wants to survive or succeed. The sociologist has to describe this desire for survival or success and, further, seek both the cause of it and the functions or consequences of it. Because the goals of the sociologist are, in a sense, more demanding, his concepts must be more precise.

Though the use of special concepts may be fruitful for the sociologist, it poses some serious problems for him. If he uses the concepts of the average man on the street, he might better come to reflect exactly how people view their world. By using the concepts of those they study, sociologists would be better able to transmit how people interpret events and objects with which they deal. This would give the sociologist better understanding of why people behave as they do.*

In using their own concepts, sociologists risk interpreting the reality of those they study quite differently than does the man being studied. The sociologist risks creating a fictional world, which has no relevance or meaning to the average citizen.

This does not dismay many sociologists, because they are not concerned with whether concepts are relevant or irrelevant to the man in the street. Most sociologists are concerned with the *utility* of concepts. They

---

* Understanding is used here in the tradition of Max Weber, who meant by the German word "verstehen" more than just a cognitive understanding. It more importantly also involves an affective understanding; it involves empathy. To understand another means that you can come to completely take the role of the other so that you know what he knows, feel what he feels, see the world as he sees it, and define elements of reality as he defines them. Understanding is thus more than a "head trip"; it is a "heart trip" also.

are concerned with whether concepts enable them to understand and predict behavior. If a concept works, in that it helps them make sense of behavior or predict behavior, then this justifies its existence, whether or not the general public recognizes the concept. There may, in fact, be no such thing as a social class, but if the idea that classes exist enables the sociologist to categorize styles of life, patterns of thought, and perception, and if it enables the sociologist to accurately predict patterns of mobility, election results, or revolution, then the sociologist will use the concept and view the world as if social classes existed.

The sociologist claims that by using concepts that differ from those used by the man on the street, he gets not only a different perspective on the world, but a better one for understanding and predicting patterns of behavior. Because of his more precise concepts, the sociologist believes he is in a better position to anticipate consequences of action and predict coming events. The use of special concepts which may not be grounded in reality creates a lively issue in contemporary sociology. Some sociologists believe that the use of special concepts is justified. Others believe that the use of concepts of those observed is the only way to accurately depict their phenomenological world.

The concepts sociologists use—social class, norms, values, society—exist in the sociologist's head. They are not real phenomena in the world, but are the sociologist's mental constructs which he abstracts from the real world. They are his tools for discussing regularities he sees.

When one uses concepts which are not inherent in reality, it is very important to speak of them as mental abstractions and not to pass them off as being part of the observed world. The analyst must not speak of social classes, for instance, as if they in fact existed.*
When abstract analytic concepts are used as if they in fact exist in reality, we call this *reification*.

VARIABLES: Concepts can be constant or variable; they can exist in one dimension, one value, or in many different dimensions. Constant concepts are unidimensional; the mental image evoked by a term implies one and only one form of an object or phenomenon. Assume that in the

---

* Evidence of the fact that social classes do not exist are the variable analyses by sociologists as to how many social classes exist in the United States, estimates ranging from two to nine with many analyses falling between these extremes. If social classes existed in fact, there would not be such variance in the analysis of social class at one time and place. Social class is a mental construct in the mind of the sociologist.

remote reaches of a distant desert, nomads see a car for the first time in their lives. It happens to be a jeep driven by some anthropologists, who explain that they are riding in a car. After the anthropologists leave, these nomads will have a constant concept of a car. The mental image which the word "car" evokes will bring to mind a singular kind of object, the one jeep they saw.

Most concepts used in sociology have several dimensions of values. We call the different qualities or dimensions of a variable concept "variables." Sex is a variable concept inasmuch as people can be male or female. Male and female are variables of the concept sex. Religion is a variable concept inasmuch as people can be Catholic, Methodist, Episcopalian, Jewish, Buddhist, etc. These denominations are variables of the concept religion. The fact that a concept may manifest itself in a variety of ways makes the term "variable" appropriate for signifying the multitude of dimensions or values of the concept. For the average American, car is not a constant concept but is a variable concept. We can distinguish cars of different manufacturers, two-door from four-door cars, hard-tops from convertibles, and so forth. While car is a concept, the variable forms which cars take—Ford, Chevrolet, Cadillac, Volkswagen—are variables of that concept.

In our everyday world, we categorize objects in terms of their color. The word "color" can include a variety of different dimensions such as the colors blue, red, yellow, orange, green, white, black, and so forth, which makes color a variable concept. The different categories of colors —red, blue, green, yellow—are variables.

It should be pointed out that not all cultures recognize the same dimensions of color. The Navaho Indians, for instance, are reputed to have no separate dimension we label as "orange". They perceive orange as a shade of yellow.

Another concept of everyday life is snow. The number of dimensions used to categorize snow often varies from individual to individual, depending upon how important snow is in a person's life. People living in areas of California or Florida, where snow is seldom seen, may be unable to categorize different types of snow. For them, snow would be a constant concept. An avid skier may depict snow as being "powder", "hard-pack" or "corn". For the skier snow is a variable concept. Like the skier, the Eskimo recognizes more dimensions of snow than does the average Californian or Floridian because snow plays a more important function in his life, and it is thus useful for him to make precise distinctions between kinds of snow.

Most Americans would have difficulty categorizing types of camels. In popular phraseology, "if you've seen one camel you've seen them all." Most Americans perceive camels to be basically alike. If nothing else, differences between camels are for all practical purposes irrelevant to us. We tend to use "camel" as if it were a constant variable. To Arab nomads, on the other hand, camels are very important, and they are reputed to have thousands of words in their vocabularies to designate different kinds of camels. These would enable the Arab to distinguish one-humped from two-humped camels, male from female camels, long-haired from short-haired camels, pregnant from non-pregnant camels, and so forth. The categories Arabs use to label camels are numerous. Unlike most Americans, Arabs treat the concept "camel" as a variable concept.

DEFINITIONS: The definition of a term is an articulation of how that term is conceptualized. It specifies the mental abstraction the researcher conjures up when he uses a term. It spells out exactly what the researcher means when he uses a term. Because concepts are man-made rather than inherent in reality, it is important that terms be explicitly defined. Different sociologists hold different conceptualizations of a common term, and thus we find that terms such as "social role", "social class", and "family" have a variety of different conceptual definitions within sociology. This may come as a surprise to beginning sociology students who are traditionally exposed to singular definitions of terms. But all terms in sociology have several conceptual definitions. By defining a term, we communicate to others the concept we have in our mind; we articulate what that term means to us.

There are two kinds of definitions which are used in sociology: nominal definitions and operational definitions. *Nominal definitions* consist of an articulation of the theoretical meaning of a term, that is, the sociologist states what his conceptualization of a term is. *Operational definitions* consist of a measurement-oriented interpretation of the nominal definition. Within most operational definitions is a description of how the term is to be measured. There must be consistency between the nominal and operational definitions of terms. If there is no such consistency, the definition of the term is said to lack *internal validity*.*

---

* Whereas internal validity usually refers to the consistency between the way terms are nominally and operationally defined, external validity refers to whether or not theoretical propositions are empirically validated when they are tested. If a proposition is validated, this reinforces our confidence in the external validity of that proposition. External validity refers to whether or not a theoretical proposition accurately describes or predicts human behavior.

Validity involves an assessment of whether a researcher is, in fact, measuring what he thinks he is measuring. If nominal and operational definitions are not consistent, then most likely the measurement instrument, derived from the operational definition, is not measuring what the researcher intends to have measured, as articulated by his nominal definition.

One of the most fruitful ways to criticize most sociological studies is to look for consistency in the nominal and operational definitions of terms. It is here that many sociologists falter. At times, there are inconsistencies in these definitions. More frequently, however, authors fail to define terms either nominally or operationally. If terms are not defined, there is no way of determining the internal validity of a measurement.

Definitions serve several functions. *Definitions aid in theory development.* One purpose of theory is to systematically interrelate theoretical propositions to convey some general pattern or process. If theoretical propositions are to be combined, they must contain logically related and internally consistent conceptual definitions.

Assume a sociologist, studying marital instability in American families, posits the theoretical proposition that "marital instability is inversely related to social class." This means that the higher the social class, the less marital instability will exist; the lower the social class, the more marital instability will exist.

Another sociologist, doing a completely different study of American family life observes that "freedom of mate choice is inversely related to social class." By this he means that people in higher social classes tend to have less freedom in selecting a mate of their choice; people in lower social classes tend to have more freedom in selecting mates of their choice.

A theorist may want to take these two propositions and combine them in a theory. In order to combine these propositions, each proposition must share logically related and internally consistent conceptual definitions. The terms which each proposition have in common must have consistent definitions. The terms which are unique to one proposition must have a logical relationship to terms in the other proposition. Thus, if these propositions were combined, social class would have the same meaning in the two propositions and marital stability and freedom of mate choice would be logically related. This interrelation would constitute yet another theoretical proposition, such as, "freedom of mate choice is positively related to instability in marriage." Two of our theoretical propositions were grounded in an empirical reality. The third proposition was derived from combining or interrelating these two. Propositions which come from logically relating two or more nominal propositions we will call derived propositions. Thus we have the beginnings of a theory of marital instability:

Nominal propositions:

1) Marital instability is inversely related to social class.
2) Freedom of mate choice is inversely related to social class.

Derived proposition:

1) Marital instability is positively related to freedom of mate choice.

It should be mentioned that when the original two studies were conducted, the nominal and operational definitions of social class may have been different in each study. To combine the two propositions, one or both of the original definitions of social class may have required change to achieve internal consistency of the definitions. The fact that definitions of concepts can be changed, enables the sociologist to build theory. It is only with this freedom that propositions specific to one time and place can be expanded upon to elaborate more general social processes.

Changing the original definition of social class would in no way affect the validity of either proposition inasmuch as each proposition in the theory has no external validity until it is empirically tested. The study which creates a theoretical proposition does not also prove the external validity of that proposition. The propositions must be continually tested and retested in a variety of times and places to gain empirical validity.

Because conceptual definitions are changeable, it is crucial that all terms be explicitly defined. Theories are composed not only of interrelated propositions but of interrelated conceptual definitions as well. Definitions are an indispensable part of all theoretical propositions, for without the conceptual definitions, we would not know what the propositions really mean.

Definitions aim and guide social research. One task of social research is to empirically test theoretical propositions. When propositions are tested, the definitions of the terms in the proposition guide the researcher in making decisions on what to measure and how to measure it. When we say that definitions aim and guide social research, we mean that every conceptual definition carries certain measurement biases within it. Every definition specifies certain aspects of a phenomenon that are relevant and important and other aspects that are presumed irrelevant or unimportant. Assume that the sociologist who observed that marital instability was inversely related to social class, defined marital instability as "the attainment of a legal divorce." This definition of marital instability articulates what measurement must be taken to test the external validity of this proposition. We must measure the concept "marital instability" by determining whether or not persons have been legally divorced. According to this definition, measurements of separation among respondents or how often respondents fight with their spouse, or whether respondents are happily married to their spouses, are irrelevant.

Where terms within theoretical propositions are clearly defined, the procedure for empirically validating that proposition is clear. Definitions convey what variables should be considered and frequently convey the kinds of measurements which should be made in validating the proposition.

EMPIRICAL INDICATORS: Empirical indicators function to link concepts to the real world. They are instruments for measuring concepts. It is through empirical indicators that concepts are operationalized. Empirical indicators can consist of one question or a series of questions within a questionnaire, interview schedule, or other research instrument. They are designed to measure a concept. The empirical indicator is derived from both the nominal and operational definitions of a term.

We have already asserted that social class is a term signifying many different concepts. When we ask how we can measure a respondent's social class or what questions we can ask people to ascertain their social class, we are looking for empirical indicators of this concept.

If social class is to be a useful concept, it must have within it some criterion for distinguishing members of one social class from members of other social classes. It assumes that a social class exists within a system of social classes. As such, a social class must be seen in terms of a larger system of which it is a part.

If we define a social class system as a hierarchy of statuses with respect to the economic processes within a society, we can use the two indices or variables most frequently used by sociologists to measure social class:

level of education and level of occupation. When these measures are used, the assessment of levels of education and occupation is usually made by some objective analyst. Information about a respondent's education or occupation comes from the respondent, but the determination of how that data are organized, and the determination of how many social classes are to be attributed to a community, is the decision of the analyst. This is called the objective approach to the study of social stratification.

If we define a social class system as a "hierarchy of statuses which is perceived to exist among selected informants in a community," we would have to go to a number of community members and ask them for their appraisals of the status hierarchy in their community. If appropriate, we might ask where specific community members were placed in their perceived hierarchy. Observation by an outside objective analyst would be inappropriate for a definition of social class, which is based on the appraisals of community members. Asking community members to assess the community's stratification system is called the reputational approach to measuring social stratification.

We could also define a social class system as "a hierarchy of statuses abstracted from appraisals of how respondents regard their own social position relative to others living in their community." Here we would ask people what social class they perceived themselves to be within. According to this definition of social class, it would be inappropriate to use either detached, objective assessors of social class or other members of the community to measure any respondent's class standing. The respondent would have to assess his own class standing. This is called the subjective approach to measuring social stratification. Note how the definition of social class will determine the type of empirical indicator to be used in measuring this term.

A very crude but valuable way of measuring social class by the objective approach is to dichotomize the empirical indicators, education and occupation, so that any individual can be classified as either high or low in level of occupation. Any person who scores high on both indicators would be classified as having high socio-economic status. Any person scoring high in one index and low on another, in any combination, can be classified as having middle socio-economic status. Any person scoring low on both indices would be classified as having low socio-economic status. This can be schemetized as follows:

How does one determine whether a person is high or low in level of education or level of occupation? If we ask a respondent for the last

		Level of Occupation	
		High	Low
Level of Education	High	High SES	Middle SES
	Low	Middle SES	Lower SES

Level of Socio-Economic Status (SES) by Level of Occupation and Level of Education

grade he was in when he last attended school, we might expect responses ranging from "I had no formal education; I never went to school" to "I completed my PhD," "I finished medical school," or "I obtained an LLD." We construct a continuum of possible educational levels and devise a cut-off point which dichotomizes the continuum into high and low educational levels. Assume we make this cut-off between high school graduation and some college. The continuum of education, when dichotomized into levels might then be:

Low level of education	No formal education 1-8 years of education Some high school High school graduate
High level of education	Some college A.A. degree (junior college graduate) some upper division college work College graduate Some graduate work MS or MA degree Beyond Ms or MA degree Ph.D., M.D., LL.D.

The person who was a high school graduate and without any college education would be scored low on level of education. The high school graduate with some college education, even though he did not have any college or junior college degree, would be scored high on level of education.

Level of occupation is harder to measure because several empirical indicators must be combined when occupations are compared. At least three factors are usually taken into account when level of occupation is measured. *Income* is one factor considered. However, income is not the only factor which sets some jobs above others. Another form of compensation for work is *prestige*. Prestige is not necessarily positively related to income. College professors, for instance, earn little income relative to the prestige of their occupation. Garbage collectors have high income relative to the prestige of their job. Jobs also differ in the amount of *power* which they afford. Power is the ability of one person to exercise his will over others. The amount of power one has in his job is often considered in assessing one's level of occupation.

Several different scales of occupational stratification have been devised by combining all three variables. One such scale, developed by the National Opinion Research Center, quantatively ranks different occupations. Numerical scores represent the result of quantifying and weighting income, power, and prestige and combining these indices into a summary score. Their scale is reproduced in Figure 1.1.

This scale is normally not dichotomized into high and low levels of occupation. It was done here because we needed dichotomous occupational categories to match our dichotomous educational categories, so that we could combine both to create an index of social class. The dichotomy for occupations was drawn at the average score for all occupations listed in the scale.

Using these indices of education and occupation, we can designate any respondent who scores high on both education and occupation as being upper socio-economic status, someone who scores high on one index and low on the other can be considered as having middle socio-economic status, and someone scoring low on both indices would be considered to have low socio-economic status.

Not all empirical indicators are as complicated as the one that was just cited. Often an empirical indicator can be simply one question. If we want to assess the age of a respondent we can ask, "How old are you?" This question is the empirical indicator of the concept "age." If we want to assess a respondent's sex, we can ask "What is your sex?" as an empirical indicator of the concept sex. Single, simple questions are not to be underrated however. They are not immune to the issue of validity. Ideally, before any empirical indicator is used, it should be compared to a plethora of alternative indices.

Figure 1.1 The Ratings of Occupations

OCCUPATION	SCORE	OCCUPATION	SCORE
U.S. Supreme Court Justice	94	Newspaper columnist	73
Physician	93	Policeman	72
Nuclear physicist	92	AVERAGE	71
Scientist	92	Reporter on a daily newspaper	71
Government scientist	91	Bookkeeper	70
State governor	91	Radio announcer	70
Cabinet member in the federal government	90	Insurance agent	69
College professor	90	Tenant farmer—one who owns livestock and machinery and manages the farm	69
U.S. Representative in Congress	90	Local official of a labor union	67
Chemist	89	Manager of a small store in a city	67
Diplomat in the U.S. Foreign Service	89	Mail carrier	66
Lawyer	89	Railroad conductor	66
Architect	88	Traveling salesman for a wholesale concern	66
County judge	88	Plumber	65
Dentist	88	Barber	63
Mayor of a large city	87	Machine operator in a factory	63
Member of the board of directors of a large corporation	87	Owner-operator of a lunch stand	63
Minister	87	Playground director	63
Psychologist	87	Corporal in the regular army	62
Airline pilot	86	Garage mechanic	62
Civil engineer	86	Truck driver	59
Head of a department in a state government	86	Fisherman who owns his own boat	58
Priest	86		

Occupation	Score
Banker	85
Biologist	85
Sociologist	83
Captain in the regular army	82
Accountant for a large business	81
Public schoolteacher	81
Building contractor	80
Owner of a factory that employs about 100 people	80
Artist who paints pictures that are exhibited in galleries	78
Author of novels	78
Economist	78
Musician in a symphony orchestra	78
Official of an international labor union	77
County agricultural agent	76
Electrician	76
Railroad engineer	76
Owner-operator of a printing shop	75
Trained machinist	75
Farm owner and operator	74
Undertaker	74
Welfare worker for a city government	74
Clerk in a store	56
Milk route man	56
Streetcar motorman	56
Lumberjack	55
Restaurant cook	55
Singer in a nightclub	54
Filling station attendant	51
Coal miner	50
Dock worker	50
Night watchman	50
Railroad section hand	50
Restaurant waiter	49
Taxi driver	49
Bartender	48
Farmhand	48
Janitor	48
Clothes presser in a laundry	45
Soda fountain clerk	44
sharecropper—one who owns no livestock or equipment and does not manage farm	42
Garbage collector	39
Street sweeper	36
Shoe shiner	34

Robert W. Hodge, Paul M. Seigel, and Peter H. Rossi, "Occupational Prestige in the United States, 1925-1963," *American Journal of Sociology*, 70 (November, 1964), 286-302. Used by permission of Professor Hodge and The University of Chicago Press.

A question should be reworded in many different ways with the advantages and disadvantages of each alternative being weighed. This is one way of improving the validity of questions; it is one way of checking to see that a question is measuring exactly what we want it to measure.

HYPOTHESES: A hypothesis is a theoretial proposition which indicates a relationship of at least two variables. The relationship between variables can be descriptive or causal. Descriptive relationships between variables exist in many forms. Two variables may co-vary. Two variables are said to co-vary in a positive relationship if, when variable X occurs, variable Y occurs also or when variable X does not occur, variable Y does not occur either. A positive relationship between variables indicates that two variables either exist or do not exist together.

Variables may co-vary in an inverse relationship. Two variables are said to be inversely related if, when variable X occurs variable Y does not occur or when variable X does not occur, variable Y does.

Variables may also be said to be positively or inversely related when the values of a variable increase or decrease relative to the values of another variable. If people, as they get older, also get more politically conservative, then age and political conservatism are positively related. As one variable increases so does the other. If people, as they get older, see a fewer number of movies each year, then age and movie viewing are inversely related. As age increases, movie going decreases. All of these examples illustrate a descriptive relation between variables in that one variable does not cause another variable to exist or not exist. Rather, one describes the quality of a relationship between variables.

A causal relation between variables exists when one variable is the cause of another. Causality is not empirically proven in sociology, but is inferred when the following conditions exist: (1) when the causal variable precedes in time the occurrence of the affected variable, (2) when the causal variable is logically related to the variable it affects, (3) when the causal variable is empirically related to the variable it is said to affect, and (4) when the causal variable, more than any other variable one tests, causes the existence of the affected variable. Causal relations will be discussed more fully in Chapter III.

All hypotheses have an implicit structure: "if..., then...". If hypotheses are not explicitly structured in this way, they can at least be translated into an "if..., then..." proposition. Factors included in the "if" part of a hypothesis specify the conditions which must exist if the hypothesis is to be applicable. These are called *independent variables*. They are factors from which a prediction is being based. The "then" part predicts what will happen when these conditions exist. Factors which are cited in the "then" part are called *dependent variables*. They are the factors which are being predicted.

At times, the independent variable does not affect the dependent variable directly. Sometimes the existence of other factors alters or affects a relationship between the independent and dependent variables. Such factors are called *intervening variables*. They are called intervening variables because they occur while the independent variable is affecting the dependent variable, and they influence the nature of the relationship between these two variables. An intervening variable is a kind of independent variable, which intervenes in time between the occurrence of an independent and dependent variable.

Whether in fact a variable is independent, intervening, or dependent, is a matter for empirical validation. Hypotheses are written as if one factor is an independent variable and another factor is a dependent variable, but the nature of the relationship between them must be empirically tested. Frequently empirical evidence reveals that what was thought to be an independent variable is in fact an intervening variable, which is not the ultimate cause of the dependent variable at all.

When a hypothesis does not predict accurately, we must discover why; we must probe for what went wrong. Hypotheses are frequently inaccurate because they are incomplete. Thus, rather than being discarded as wrong, hypotheses are often refined. This refinement frequently involves adding additional independent or intervening variables to the hypothesis. If a hypothesis has no empirical validity, the sociologist must alter it to make it reflect the empirical world. An example of how this is done is in order.

During the depression several studies were done which focused on the effects of unemployment on family life. These studies indicated that "if a man becomes unemployed, then he will lose considerable authority in his home." Among the reasons given for this hypothesis was that the base of the man's authority was his ability to provide for the physical needs of his family. Being economically dependent upon the husband, the other family members acquiesced to the traditional patriarchal pattern of authority. With unemployment, the base of the husband's authority crumbled. He was no longer able to supply the family with the necessities of life. His own self-respect and the respect of other family members for him was undermined, and the husband experienced a decline in the willingness of the family to accept his control.

Though this formulation seems reasonable and logically sound, it is nevertheless incomplete. The hypothesis was refined by Mirra Komarovsky, who found that it was not accurate for some of the families she observed during the depression.[3]

She found that unemployment did not destroy the husband's authority in some families. She asked what the difference was between the families for which the hypothesis did and did not hold true.

She found the significant difference to be the nature of the foundation on which the marriage was based. Some marriages operated around social roles which family members performed. Members were evaluated on the basis of what they did, on the basis of what functions they served for the family. People were loved because they were good providers, good football players, impressive scholars, or successful socialities. They were loved because of things they did, not because of who they were. Marriages which are based on functional contingencies are said to be based on *instrumental* considerations. In these marriages, unemployment seriously affected a husband's authority.

Other marriages were based on *expressive* considerations. People were loved because of who they were, not because of things they did or did not do. Unemployment had little or no effect in undermining the husband's authority in these families. The husband was basically the same man whether he was working or not and he was loved and respected regardless of his employment status.

This is an overly simplified account of Komarovsky's findings. Other variables such as the kind of authority patterns that existed prior to the unemployment and the way the unemployment was rationalized (whether it was the husband's or the system's fault) also affected change in authority patterns.

What is important is that a hypothesis existed which did not fit an empirical reality. The hypothesis "if a man becomes unemployed then he will lose considerable authority in his home" was true only some of the time. It was refined to fit the empirical world. The revised hypothesis read, "if a man becomes unemployed *and* his marriage is based on instrumental considerations, then he will lose considerable authority in his home." An addition was made to the "if" part of the hypothesis.

---

[3] Mirra Komarovsky, *The Unemployed Man and His Family* (New York: Dryden Press, 1940).

As independent and intervening variables are added to a hypothesis to refine it, the range of applicability for that hypothesis is reduced. Hypotheses exist at many different ranges of applicability. The higher the range of a hypothesis, the more people, situations, times, and places are incorporated within that hypothesis. The more people, situations, times and places that are incorporated within any theoretical proposition, including a hypothesis, the higher is that proposition's *level of abstraction*.

We can illustrate how single hypotheses can exist at many different levels of abstraction by means of an outline model.

I. Minority groups will have less power than majority groups in a society.
  A. Racial minority groups will have less power than racial majority groups in a society.
    1. Black people living within the United States, will have less power than Caucasians living within the United States.
    2. Orientals living within the United States will have less power than Caucasians living within the United States.
      a. Chinese people living within the United States will have less power than Caucasians living within the United States.
      b. Japanese people living within the United States will have less power than Caucasians living within the United States.
  B. Religious minority groups will have less power than religious majority groups in a society.
    1. Catholics living within the United States will have less power than Protestants living within the United States.
    2. Jews living within the United States will have less power than Protestants living within the United States.

There are four levels of abstraction reflected in the above set of hypotheses. The hypothesis labeled I is the highest level of abstraction in this sequence and incorporates within it all the other hypotheses. It includes all minority groups, whether they be racial, ethnic, or social minority groups. Statement A is included within statement I because it includes a special category of minority groups, racial minorities. Statements 1 and 2 are of a lower order than is statement A because they include special sub-categories of proposition A, namely, two types of racial minorities. Statements a and b are subsumed under statement 2 because they constitute two different oriental cultures which exist within American society.

Statement B is of the same level of abstraction as statement A. Both statements are predicting about categories of minority group, racial and religious minorities. Statement B-1 is of the same level of abstraction as is statement A-1 in that it has the same logical position in the structure as does statement A-1. Actually, from a somewhat different perspective, if there are more Catholics than Blacks in the United States, then statement B-1 has a slightly greater range inasmuch as it is predicting for a greater number of people. Statement B-2 is of the same level of abstraction in this scheme as statements A-1, A-2, or B-2.

Once all concepts are defined, empirical indicators can be devised for measuring the concepts, and the hypotheses can be tested. It is probably easier and less costly to test the lowest level hypotheses because the population to be studied is smaller, more homogeneous and more clearly delimited. Note that in the structure we have outlined, the failure to validate a low level hypothesis seriously affects all higher level hypotheses. If it is not true that "Japanese living in the United States will have less power than Caucasians living in the United States," we would seriously question whether it is true that "Orientals living in the United States will have less power than Caucasians living in the United States," and that "racial minority groups will have less power than racial majority groups in a society," and that "minority groups will have less power than majority groups in a society." The testing of a low level hypothesis reflects on the validity of all higher level hypotheses which are logically related to the tested hypotheses.

If a power level statement is false the higher level statement is not automatically also false. Though Japanese in the United States may be found empirically to have more power than Caucasians, it may still be true that Orientals living in the United States have less power than Caucasians, if the Japanese consistute a small enough sub-system of Orientals. A hypothesis need not be 100% correct to be empirically validated. Researchers select the criterion by which a hypothesis is accepted as valid or not, and this criterion may be that the hypothesis is correct 100%, 90%, 80% or 51% of the time. For this reason it is possible for statement I-A-2-b to be empirically false and for statement I-A-2 to be empirically validated.

High level hypotheses are generally considered to have higher level explanatory power than lower level hypotheses. They are thought to have higher explanatory power because the range of phenomena they take into account is much greater than that of lower level hypotheses.

Though the empirical validation of high level hypotheses would give a social scientist a great deal of explanatory and predictive power, the fact remains that the higher the level of a hypothesis, the more difficult it becomes to empirically validate it. The higher the level of the hypothesis, the more hypotheses there are subsumed under it, which, when tested, could invalidate or force an alteration of the higher level hypothesis.

There is such diversity in the kinds of groups and the kinds of social settings in a society that high level hypotheses usually fail to be validated because they are too simple, too incomplete. They fail to be validated because they fail to take into account the complex diversity of human group life. Once this diversity is taken into account in a hypothesis, there are so many variables included in a hypothesis that it is no longer a high level hypothesis.

A dilemma is thus presented to the social scientist. He would like to create and validate high level hypotheses because they have such high explanatory power, yet the empirical world is too diverse and high level hypotheses do not fit this complex world. Low level hypotheses take into account diversity and complexity and predict behavior accurately but for only a small number of persons in a very limited number of social settings. The social scientist thus has a choice of continuing to create and trying to validate high level hypotheses, the vast majority of which will not be validated, or to work within the limited though surer bounds of low level hypotheses. This dilemma is a central issue of contemporary sociology.

THEORIES: A theory is a system of logically related, logically complete, internally consistent definitions and hypotheses. Each hypothesis that is part of a theory must ideally meet the following conditions:

1. *Each hypothesis must be empirically verifiable.*
Each hypothesis must be capable of being tested. Theories are not tested directly. Rather each hypothesis within a theory is tested. If all hypotheses are empirically validated, one gains considerable confidence in the validity of the overall theory. Theories that contain hypotheses which are repeatedly validated when empirically tested become *laws*. Laws, then, are theories which contain repeatedly tested and validated hypotheses. A theory does not become a law until one is confident of the theory's empirical external validity.

2. *Each hypothesis must be couched in exactly defined terms.*
In order to be verifiable, hypotheses must contain terms which are explicitly defined. Only then can appropriate operational definitions of concepts be devised and the hypothesis be validly tested.

3. *All hypotheses must be consistent with one another.*
Hypotheses must be logically consistent. There must be no two hypotheses which imply contradictory things. Two contradictory statements cannot both work to support a higher level generalization.

4. *Hypotheses which constitute a theory must be logically complete.*
There must be no steps left out which would prevent one from moving from a hypothesis at one level of abstraction to a hypothesis at another level, whether this be a higher or lower level. The hypotheses must be logically related to one another.

To illustrate a theory, we borrow the basic thesis of Emile Durkheim's classic study of *Suicide*.[4]
Our theory consists of three basic hypotheses:

1. Catholics exhibit lower suicide rates than do Protestants.

2. Catholics are more highly integrated into the social structure than are Protestants.

3. The more groups are integrated into the social structure, the lower will be their rates of suicide.

For these hypotheses to be tested, all concepts must be nominally and operationally defined. Nominal and operational definitions necessary to test these hypotheses are offered below. The nominal definition of each concept is given first, followed by an operational definition of that concept.

Catholic -	A follower of the Catholic Church. A person who states that his religion is Catholic.
Protestant -	A follower of some Protestant Church. A person who states that his religion is some Protestant denomination.

---

[4] Emile Durkheim, *Suicide. A Study in Sociology*. Translated by John A. Spaulding and George Simpson (New York: Free Press of Glencoe, 1951).

Integrated -	Involvement in collective activity. Number of hours per day spent in social interaction with other adults.
Social Structure -	The parts of a social system. The network of social institutions in a society.
Suicide Rate -	A measure of suicide frequency. The number of suicides divided by the total population sharing some characteristic, this quotient to be multiplied by 1000.
Group -	A social aggregate of persons. Persons having a designated characteristic in common.

The term suicide would also have to be defined. Durkheim defined it as "all cases of death resulting directly or indirectly from a positive or negative act of the victim himself, which he knows will produce this result." In adding the last clause of his definition, Durkheim gives his definition a cognitive bias. The suicide victim must recognize, must realize that his action will result in his death. The person who dies from an overdose of drugs would not be considered a suicide victim if he did not anticipate that he might die when he took the drugs.

We have taken our nominal definition of integration directly from Durkheim. Durkheim was trying to demonstrate that differential suicide rates in different countries were not a function of weather or geography or psychological factors, but of empirically observable social factors. His exposition of just what "involvement in collective activity" means is left rather ambiguous, as he fails, for instance, to distinguish collective activity in business and in leisure. When Durkheim explains higher suicide rates during working hours than in the evening, he seems to imply that collective activity means business activity. But in his explanation of greater suicide rates during holidays, such as Christmas and Easter, collective activity seems to mean leisure activity. We imply in our definition that collective activity combines business and leisure activity, and we hope that this will not lead to ambiguities as it did for Durkheim.

The entire structure of interrelated definitions and hypotheses outlined above constitutes a sociological theory. One way of checking to see how many hypotheses are required for a theory is to construct a matrix of the concepts within the theory. Each concept must be linked to all the other concepts in a theory by a hypothesis. In the theory above, there are three concepts, religion, suicide rate and social integration. We construct a matrix of these concepts as follows:

	Religion	Suicide Rate	Social Integration
Religion		1	2
Suicide Rate			3
Social Integration			

Concepts are arranged in the same order along both axes of the matrix. One does not interrelate a concept to itself, thus a line is drawn through the intersection of a concept with itself. This line will bisect the table. One goes across the matrix numbering each empty cell of the matrix *above* the line which bisects the table. Each cell indicates the need for a hypothesis to link the concepts which that cell intersects. The matrix for our theory shows a need for three propositions. Proposition 1 requires a linkage of religion and suicide rates. Proposition 2 requires a linkage of religion and social integration. Proposition 3 requires a linkage of suicide rates and social integration. As this matrix indicates, to be logically complete, every concept in a theory must be related to all other concepts in the theory through a separate proposition. To be logically consistent and complete, variables of each concept in each hypothesis must also be related to all other variables in the total theoretical structure.

If we were to empirically validate the hypothesis: Catholics exhibit lower suicide rates than do Protestants, we would have to measure the terms "Catholic" "suicide rate" and "Protestant". To measure these terms, we would have to construct empirical indicators for these terms, and to do this, we must look to their operational definitions. Looking at the operational definition of Catholic as given in the theory, we see that two empirical indicators are needed to measure this term: what do (did) you (he) consider to be your (his) religion? and Did you (he) attend a Catholic Church function at least twice in the past year? The words in parentheses would be asked about recent suicide victims. The testing of any hypothesis involves the measuring of terms within that hypothesis. Measuring terms involves constructing empirical indicators of the concepts those terms signify. These concepts are articulated in the definitions of those terms. Definitions guide us in operationalizing the terms in a hypothesis. Hypotheses and definitions are thus integral and necessary elements of all theories, for without them, the theories could never be evaluated through the testing of its hypotheses.

CHAPTER 2

MEASUREMENT AND THEORY CREATION

The main task of sociology is to construct accurate generalizations which describe and account for regularities of human group life. These generalizations are sociological theories.

The purpose of measurement in sociology is to create and test sociological theory. Creating theory and testing theory are two different but related enterprises. In this chapter we will examine how theories are created through measurement. In the next chapter we will examine how theories are evaluated through measurement.

There are four basic research designs in sociology: field work, survey research, laboratory experimentation, and document analysis.

Most hypotheses in sociology have come out of research which has had a field work or survey research design. In illustrating how hypotheses are created and combined to make theories, it is appropriate that we discuss these two designs and then illustrate how they can be used to create hypotheses and theories.

CREATING THEORY WITH FIELD WORK

Field work involves observing human group life in natural settings. This means that if a researcher wants to know what policemen do during a normal patrol, they will go with policemen and observe them as the police perform their normal duties. If a researcher wants to know what life is like for the black, urban, ghetto-dwelling male, he will live with them, go where they go, and observe them. If a researcher wants to know what life is like in a small midwestern town, or in a prison, or in a department of some organization, he will not just ask people working in these places what their life is like. He will go directly to these settings, experience this life himself, and in addition, will talk to people in these settings to get their perspectives and feelings about what their life and environment is like. The field worker not only seeks knowledge about a social setting or group of people, but he further seeks a subjective feeling for the settings and people he studies. He seeks to truly understand them, and to come to grips with what those observed think and feel.

Field work has long been the basic research technique of anthropologists, who would observe and study small, homogeneous so-called primitive societies. The anthropologist would live with the people he observed, interview them, talk with them, accompany them wherever he could, and in as many ways as possible integrate himself into their society.

The sociologist who does field work usually does not study whole societies. He examines smaller units such as communities, organizations, small groups, or subcultures. The sociologist is usually interested in describing either the structure of the unit to be studied (how it is organized), or the ordinary, normal, taken-for-granted routines of everyday life in a specific setting. In this respect, the sociologist as field worker differs very much from the journalist, who seeks the sensational and unique occurrences to write about. One focus of contemporary urban sociology is to study the everyday worlds of people constituting diverse urban subcultures: prostitutes, police, alcoholics, criminals, morticians, cab drivers, homosexuals, and many others. One reason for observing recurrent, everyday behavior is that, because it happens every day, over and over again, it is worth understanding.

Observation, which is the central task of field workers, usually exists in two forms: direct observation and participant observation. In *direct observation*, the researcher is not a part of what he observes. He remains aloof, on the sidelines, so to speak, and observes behavior and events. He can be physically present at the scene as one might be if observing political rallies or police on patrol. He can also be one step removed from the observed scene as one would be if, through a one-way mirror, he viewed children playing or if, by means of hidden video-tape equipment or tape recorders, he observed families interacting.

In *participant observation*, the researcher plays an active part in the events which he is observing. The fact that the observer is a part of the scene he observes makes it very difficult for the participant observer to be objective. Through his involvement, he comes to internalize perceptions and definitions of objects and events from others. He comes to identify with some factions and dislike others. This loss of objectivity is a risk of participant observation.

The advantage in being a participant on the scene is that the observer gets a deep subjective feeling for what it is like to be a part of the events, organization or setting which is the object of study. He gets this insight by being himself subjected to the same pressures, frustrations, problems, rewards and pleasures as others. He also gets insights from others with whom he associates. His close interaction with those he observes gives him access to their feelings, perceptions, and opinions.

An issue which is applicable to both direct and participant observation is whether or not those who are being observed should know that they are being observed. What are the advantages and disadvantages of their knowing?

It is sometimes feared that if subjects know they are being observed, they are apt to put on a "front" which they would not if they did not know they were being observed. Fronts are patterns of behavior designed to convey an image; they ameliorate what normatively occurs in a given setting.

Bureaucracies, for instance, usually operate on two different levels, a formal and an informal level. The formal level is depicted in organizational charts and in staff manuals. These formal charts and manuals constitute a type of front for public consumption. These formal charts and manuals frequently do not tell what "really" happens in an organization. In the informal proceedings, it might be that secretaries, wives, friends, or junior executives make many of the decisions that are attributed to high officials. Where it is official that coffee breaks are 15 minutes in length and lunch breaks one hour, it may be that, in fact, they last much longer for some people.

In many social settings, there is a difference between what people want you to think is happening and what is really happening in that setting. Fronts are intended to prevent the observer from discovering what really happens, which is, of course, exactly what the observer wants to know. It is thus the task of the field worker to break through these fronts so that he can come to understand what normatively occurs.

Front behavior is much more a matter of concern to the observer who is doing short term observation than it is to one who is observing a setting or organization over an extended time. The longer a researcher observes within a social setting, the more fronts he will be able to see through. He will be able to see through fronts because it is difficult for groups to maintain front behavior over long periods of time. Most social groups operate within very routinized behavior patterns. It is very difficult to alter normative behavior for the benefit of the observer for long periods of time wthout seriously affecting the ability of the group to function smoothly.

The longer we spend with persons, the more we gain their confidence that we are genuine. There is never any guarantee that observed behavior will not be front behavior, but the longer a researcher works with a group, the more he will be trusted, and the more difficult it will be for the group to maintain a front.

Another argument for the contention that subjects should not know that they are being observed is not that they will establish fronts, but that their normative behavior will be somehow altered by this knowledge. They may, for instance, become more inhibited, more cautious.

The contention that knowing one is being observed will inhibit one's actions runs contrary to my experience. I have observed families who know their interaction is being video-taped and tape recorded. They interact around a table in the center of which is a microphone in plain view. Despite this they are able to build up such emotional tension that individual members become so distraught that they are unable to continue. They emotionally "flood out", either by crying or laughing hysterically, or by becoming so angry that they are unable to continue. If observation had any inhibiting effect on any of these individuals, this kind of behavior would never have occurred. Once again time usually comes to the researcher's aid. When people know they are being observed, they may become inhibited or cautious for a short time, but eventually, this is lost and there is every reason to believe that the observer is seeing normative behavior.

It is very tempting for the observer to try to conceal his role. For instance, I know of a graduate student who wanted to study the everyday dynamics of family life, who proposed to work for a family as a live-in babysitter-housekeeper, as a means of gaining access to a family to obtain data. She had no intention of telling the family she was there for ulterior motives. I also know of a student who proposed to join a commune so as to obtain data on it, without telling anyone in the commune that she was there to observe them. These breeches of a professional ethic are fraught with dangers for both the researcher and the observed.

The risk for the observed is that they have no opportunity to review the observations or the presentation of the findings. Once these are released, there is little control over the consequences of the research for those observed. Research findings which reveal informal procedures or statements from those observed can wreak havoc within the setting, particularly when anonymity is not preserved carefully enough.

The risks to the observer are multiple. He risks alienating the observed group and takes the chance that anyone even remotely connected with those observed will never again cooperate with anyone doing social science research. The person who conducts research must recognize that he represents not only himself, but an entire enterprise. He must be careful not to destroy his territory for other social scientists who might want to replicate his work or conduct other forms of research.

A further risk to the observer is that, in order to preserve his secrecy, he cannot communicate about his findings with any of those observed. The risk here is that he has no check against his misinterpreting what he observes and has no access to additional information which might elaborate on and embellish some skeletal ideas. It is important to discuss one's research findings with respondents so that they have an opportunity to verify, add to, refute or discuss them. Often their comments can save embarrassment to both those observed and the researcher. Sometimes they point out that the researcher has given away too many clews to the identity of respondents. Sometimes they show how the researcher has misinterpreted an event or left something incomplete in his analysis.

In field work there is no need for secrecy. When respondents are openly confronted with a research proposal, more frequently than one might expect, they are flattered at being selected as an object of study, are impressed by the researcher's openness, and accept the research. There is no reason for secrecy because after a short time, the observer does not alter normative patterns of behavior, even when people know they are being observed. Secrecy is just not worth the risks that are inherent within it.

DATA COLLECTION: Observation can be conducted with instruments as simple as a pencil and a piece of paper or as complex as a tape-recorder, movie camera, or video tape unit.

A simple observational technique which is widely used by anthropologists and sociologists involves observing events and behavior for a time and then leaving the field to write down notes of what the observer remembers seeing. This has the advantage of not taking notes in plain view at the scene. By not taking notes, the observer can blend into the scene he is observing and is less apt to affect the flow of events. The key to success in this technique is not to wait too long after gaining a significant insight to record it. Much detail and accuracy is lost in time. Sometimes whole ideas are forgotten if the researcher waits too long to record them. The measurements that are obtained through this technique tend to be qualitative and sometimes impressionistic, rather than statistical. This in no way reduces their value. This technique just produces a particular type of data.

An alternative technique is to record data as it occurs. This involves taking notes or tallying scores on paper or reading into a tape recorder while at the scene. Here statistical data can be obtained from whatever scorekeeping is done. The advantage of this is that data can be recorded immediately after an observed event occurs. One must be careful, however, when recording events, that subsequent events are not missed while notes are being written, and that the obvious recording of data does not affect behavior which is being observed.

An example of the detail which can be recorded with direct observation is given by Barker and his associates in their book *One Boy's Day*. They collected their data through a combination of written notes and taped observations. An example of their notes for one minute of behavior is given below. The minute is between 7:00 and 7:01 am and describes the beginning of the boy's getting up.[5]

> 7:00 Mrs. Birch said with pleasant casualness, "Raymond, wake up." With a little more urgency in her voice she spoke again: "Son, are you going to school today?"
>
> Raymond didn't respond immediately.
>
> He screwed up his face and whimpered a little.
>
> He lay still.
>
> His mother repeated, "Raymond, wake up." This was said pleasantly; the mother was apparently in good spirits and was willing to put up with her son's reluctance.
>
> Raymond whimpered again, and kicked his feet rapidly in protest.
>
> He squirmed around and rolled over crossways on the bed.
>
> His mother removed the covers.
>
> *Raymond wore a T-shirt and pajama pants.*
>
> He again kicked his feet in protest.
>
> He sat up and rubbed his eyes.

---

[5] Roger Barker and Herbert F. Wright, *One Boy's Day* (New York, Harper, 1951).

He glanced at me and smiled.

I smiled in return as I continued making notes.

> Mrs. Birch took some clothes from the bureau and laid them on the bed next to Raymond. There were a clean pair of socks, a clean pair of shorts, a white T-shirt and a striped T-shirt. Raymond's blue-jean pants were on a chair near the bed. Mrs. Birch continued to stand beside the bed.

To avoid any confusion, Barker and his associates limited only one single action to each paragraph. A new action merited a new paragraph. Italicized passages consist of extended interpretative comments by the observer and are not an actual recording of behavior. The detail which is reflected in these observations is impressive. This account shows how much data can be collected with relatively limited resources.

The reader may be struck by the amount of interpretation that is included in this description of behavior. This interpretation is needed to help make sense of what is happening. Descriptions of behavior must be multi-dimensional. One cannot give an account just of the words that people say and one cannot describe just a person's bodily movements. Neither by itself is complete enough to present a context for interpreting a stream of behavior. If a transcript were presented of only verbal conversation, it would be very difficult to interpret. The reader would have to fill in all the pitch, resonance, intensity and inflections which reflect the mood of the actor. If moods of actors are recorded and if apparent motives of action are stated, behavior can be more fully understood. Furthermore, with the recorder making the observations on the scene, there is less likelihood of misinterpreting behavior.

Barker gives us a good indication of how much diverse information is needed to fully understand a situation when he describes action and the environment in which it occurs. When it states, for instance, that the boy "walked out behind the house until he stood just west of the clothesline facing the barn" or that he "walked on the ledge around the well by the sidewalk", it is difficult for us to picture in our mind what the scene really looked like. Barker supplies pictures of these settings and it makes the reader very aware of how inadequate the written word is in describing phenomena. The best way to record observational material is to take a video tape or sound film of the data. The observers thus have maximal visual and auditory input by which to comprehend and interpret behavior. The data is not lost after a single occurrence in that it can be played back for further analysis, review, or for checking systematized measurement. The data taken is rich in detail and can be used for a wide variety of measurements.

A less efficient medium for presenting data is a tape recording or a silent movie. If a tape recording is used, all visual data are lost. If a silent movie is used, all auitory data are lost. The loss of either cuts out a tremendous body of information which gives meaning to both the entire scene and its component parts. Written transcripts of interaction are sometimes used for data but here a great deal of information must be supplied by conjecture of the reader, including mood, delivery, gestures, etc.

The least rich method of data collection is note taking, in all its varied forms. Once raw data occurs, it is lost if the observer has not recorded it completely. The form of measurement is furthermore somewhat limited by the type of notes and the amount of information the researcher gathers. The ability to use the data for a variety of purposes is reduced relative to other, more elaborate ways of recording events.

With films, tapes, and video-tapes being so useful in social research, a word must be said about the gains and pitfalls of using this electronic equipment.

Tape recorders are used to capture verbal data which can be played back and analyzed in detail over and over again. Sociologists who study families, for instance, can learn a great deal about interaction by listening to a family's dinner table conversation. Once these conversations are recorded, a group of judges analyzes the tape, looking for such things as coalition patterns, frequencies of who talks most and least, interruption patterns, leadership patterns, roles which are played, etc. Tape recorders have also been used to observe pattens in political rallies on college campuses, to record interviews, and to record patterns of meetings or conferences.

When using tape recorders, the principle problem lies in making comprehensible what the researcher wants to record and eliminating all other background noise. This is made somewhat easier by the existence of unidirectional microphones, yet it is surprising how much background noise is present to interfere with tape recording. Because of noise, outdoor recording is particularly difficult.

The use of tape recorders to conduct social research has been made easier with the development of light-weight, portable tape recorders with unidirectional microphones These are extremely expensive machines, but they make the use of tape recorders practicable to an extent hitherto impossible.

Observation work done by filming or video-taping is even more expensive, but the material obtained is extremely rich. Whereas tape recording allows an observer to capture communicative phenomena such as tone of voice, who speaks how often, what is said, etc., it does not record gestures, non-verbal messages, seating arrangements, or the appearance of actors, and this type of information is sometimes very valuable in interpreting interaction.

AN EXERCISE IN CREATING THEORY: Field work can be an effective design for creating hypotheses and theories. An exercise which I have effectively used with students involves their going to some well-defined, boundary-maintained public setting. Their job is to observe human behavior in that setting. Some students are sent to observe behavior in public elevators, some observe behavior in public restrooms, some observe at soda-fountain counters, some are sent to public waiting rooms in bus depots, train stations, or hospitals, some observe behavior on buses and trains. If a student opts for one kind of setting, he must go to several different elevators, or restrooms, or soda-fountain counters. He must observe in his setting at different times of the day or night. His job is to create a set of hypotheses which will accurately predict human behavior in his setting over different times and places.

What the student must do to create the hypotheses is get a feeling for regularities of behavior occurring in his setting. His hypotheses assume that the behavioral regularities which he observed in the past will continue to occur in the future.

The class is broken into small gros. All members of a group go to the same setting. Each group is assigned a different setting. After the hypotheses are devised, the groups meet and share their observations. They confirm or disconfirm each others' observations from their experience in that setting and come up with a collective series of hypotheses which they feel are applicable to their setting. The hypotheses are recorded for every group, and the class sees if any hypotheses seem to apply for all social settings. They thus create a hierarchy of hypotheses. Some hypotheses will be applicable to all public places and some will only be applicable to specific settings.

One of the first things the student learns when he enters the field to observe is that he cannot be a pure observer. Direct observation and participant observation are not necessarily mutually exclusive approaches; they are ideal types that constitute polar ends of a continuum of observation. When an observer is in a public setting, he must abide by the rules of that setting, which means he must engage in behavior appropriate to that setting. If he goes into a public restroom, he must use that restroom. It violates the rules of restroom behavior to stand around and watch others; behavior in public restrooms must be purposeful. If one sits at a soda-fountain counter he is expected to order at least a cup of coffee. The observer must, to some extent, be a participant in the scene he observes. Pure direct observation is limited to those who are apart from the observed scene, those who are out of sight behind a one-way mirror or in another room.

As the student begins to observe, he begins to feel very lost. The world seems to be composed of a myriad of unconnected, meaningless acts. By having to create hypotheses, the student becomes painfully aware of the role of hypotheses in social research. Hypotheses impose a structure on the empirical world so that this world becomes more comprehensible. Hypotheses structure the observer's focus of attention; they give the observer direction in assessing what is and what is not relevant data. Without hypotheses to guide one's research, the observer must try to record anything and everything.

This is not nearly as easy as it sounds. How does one organize observations? How does one structure his data? How does one know what to look at and what to ignore? Roger Barker discusses these questions in his book, *The Stream of Behavior*.[6]

If one is testing hypotheses, the hypotheses structure our observations of the world. Hypotheses are composed of concepts which specify classes of objects and events. The dimensions or values of a concept are the variables of this concept. Variables cut up the world into analytic categories, which Barker calls "tesserae." Tesserae are theoretically-created parts of the empirical world. They are created by the categories, the variables, a sociologist uses to analyze the world.

If one does not have pre-set variables with which to structure his observations, according to Barker, the world presents its own "natural units" which can be used to structure observation. The natural units

---

[6] Roger Barker, ed. *The Stream of Behavior* (New York: Appleton Century-Croft, 1963).

which Barker uses exist along a time dimension. In describing a day in the life of a boy, Barker and his associates divided the day into what they considered to be natural time units: before school, morning at school, noon hour, afternoon at school, after-school play, and evening at home. Each time unit was further divided into sub-units. Morning at home, for instance, consists of various scenes including getting up, breakfast, indoor activity, and outdoor play. Barker maintains that the use of natural units provides a more accurate depiction of the real world than does the use of tesserae. Natural units come out of the empirical world. Tesserae often do not. Tesserae are theoretically created units of analysis that might not fit an empirical situation well.

The use of natural units to structure observation is made difficult by the fact that one must segment a stream of continuous behavior into stages. The world is not, in fact, divided into stages. This makes establishing clear-cut boundaries between stages an extremely difficult task.

To show how difficult it can be to establish natural units within a stream of behavior, we will analyze a date involving John and Marcia who are going to a theatre performance. We will divide their data into three natural time units: before theatre, at the theatre, after theatre. At what point does the "before theatre" start? Does it start when John and Marcia are first born, when John first meets Marcia, when John first has the idea of asking Marcia to the theatre, when John actually asks Marcia to the theatre, when Marcia accepts John's invitation, when John buys the theatre tickets, when John begins getting dressed for his date or when Marcia begins getting dressed, when John rings Marcia's doorbell or when Marcia opens her door, when they start driving to the theatre or when they start walking to the theatre from their parked car? When does the stage "before theatre" end and the stage "at the theatre" begin? Are they "at the theatre" when they park their car in a parking lot near the theatre, when they arrive at the theatre box office to pick up their tickets, when they are handed their tickets, when they enter the theatre door, when they get to their seats, or when the lights dim? Natural units are not easily arrived at because reality exists as a continuous stream of behavior and events and does not divide itself up into neat stages. Stage boundaries are imposed by an observer; they do not come as naturally as Barker would have us believe.

Furthermore, time is not the only dimension around which natural units can be organized. The world can be structured in space as well as in time. The students whom I sent to observe public settings generally found it easier to organize their observations in terms of space than time. Many tended to divide their setting into spatial territories. They then describe activities occurring in these territories and showed how activities occurring in one territory were linked to activities occurring in other territories. Restrooms, for instance, could be divided into urinal areas, stall areas, washbasin areas, empty space areas, or lounge areas.

One very fruitful theory of human behavior in public places which my students came upon dealt with the issue of how people organize themselves in space. To illustrate how theories can be created from field work, I present an account of how this theory came to be.

A student is studying elevator behavior. He is insightful, and observes that people entering elevators regularly head for the sides, not the middle of the car. He observes that all people, after entering the car, turn around and face the doors of the elevator rather than standing in the car as they entered it, with their backs to the door. He observes that people in elevators tend to maximize the distance between themselves and others already occupying the car. He also notes that people in an elevator do not look at one another but focus their attention on the floor, door, or level indicator. These observations can be couched in a number of hypotheses:

1) People entering an elevator will, if possible, stand against a wall of the elevator rather than stand in the middle of the elevator.
2) Persons entering an elevator will face the door of the elevator rather than the back wall.
3) Persons entering an elevator will maximize the distance between themselves and others already occupying the car.
4) People in an elevator will avoid looking at other persons occupying that elevator.

Upon hearing hypothesis three, a student, who had observed behavior at soda fountain counters, voices his observation that this spacing behavior operated in his setting too. He observed that if there were two people sitting at a counter with seats separating them, then a third party would sit roughly equidistant between them, rather than sitting right next to someone. If there are three seats separating two occupants, for instance, the third party will invariably sit in the middle seat, thereby maximizing the distance between himself and others. Spacing behavior is a phenomenon of soda fountain counters too.

At this time a student studying restroom behavior voices his observa-

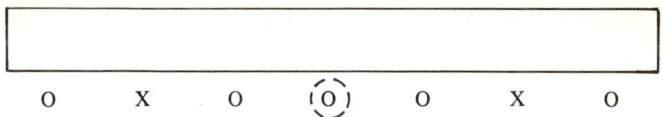

Figure 2.1. Spacing Behavior at a Soda Fountain Counter. X is occupied seat. Next occupant will space himself by using circled seat.

tion that spacing behavior also exists in his setting. Upon entering a restroom, people will try to avoid using stalls or urinals which are already occupied. People will maximize the distance between themselves and others in restrooms too.

Three hypotheses have been created:
1) Persons entering an elevator will engage in spacing behavior.
2) Persons seating themselves at a soda-fountain counter will engage in spacing behavior.
3) Persons approaching restroom facilities will engage in spacing behavior.

All three of these hypotheses exist at the same level of abstraction. Another hypothesis could be created at a higher level of abstraction which would encompass all three of these hypotheses, namely that persons in public places will engage in spacing behavior. Hypotheses have been created at different levels of abstraction but no theory yet exists to account for this behavior. No theory exists because we do not yet have at least three concepts which are interrelated to each other in a system of hypotheses and definitions.

To make an explanatory theory which will account for these observations, empirically testable hypotheses which would account for spacing behavior had to be devised. These explanatory hypotheses, when combined with the empirical observation of spacing, resulted in an explanatory theory of spacing behavior. Such a theory follows:

1) If people are in public places then they will engage in spacing behavior.
2) If people are in public places, then they will want privacy.
3) If people want privacy, then they will engage in spacing behavior.

A. Nominal definitions:

Public places - social settings to which admittance is not a function of membership restrictions.

Engage in spacing behavior - maximizing the distance between oneself and others in a setting.

Want privacy - preferring to avoid social interaction with others.

Another explanatory theory which could be created from collective observations is:

1) If people are in public places, then they will not exchange glances with others.

2) If people are in public places, then they will want privacy.

3) If people want privacy, then they wil not exchange glances with others.

Nominal definitions:

Public places - social settings to which admittance is not a function of membership restrictions.

Not exchange glances with others - not having one's visual field intersect with someone else's.

Want privacy. - preferring to avoid social interaction with others.

Want privacy. - preferring to avoid social interaction with others.

These are examples of inductive theory building. *Inductive theory building* involves starting with small-scale, empirically grounded observations which are combined with larger-scale observations to create higher level abstract generalizations. The converse of inductive theory building is deductive theory building. *Deductive theory building* involves making an initial high level generalization and then deducing from that, lower level generalizations. Had we started with the observation that people who seek privacy will maximize the distance between themselves and others, we could deduce from this that in public places, people would space themselves and that they would do this to insure maximum privacy.

The theories which these students created are not new. The foundations of these theories were laid by Erving Goffman in his book *Behavior in Public Places*.[7]

However, for my students, this was a creative enterprise.

Their theories, if correct, point out an apparent paradox of everyday life. What we call public places are really places where people are most concerned about maximizing their privacy. In public places, most people are strangers to one another. Furthermore, most people seem to want to remain anonymous strangers. The norms of a public setting prohibit one from engaging another in conversation or touching another without good reason.

---

[7] Erving Goffman, *Behavior in Public Places* (Glencoe: Free Press, 1963).

The theories indicating that public places are really privatized places have a good deal of explanatory power. They allow us to understand why people space themselves. They space themselves to avoid physical or social contact with others. The second theory allows us to understand why people in elevators all face the same way - toward the door. If everyone is faced in the same direction, whether in an elevator or at a soda fountain counter, the likelihood is reduced that people will exchange visual glances which might lead to social interaction. This is also why people do not look at each other. An exchange of visual fields is often a precursor to interaction. The theory even helps us to understand why so frequently, urinals and sinks in restrooms are against walls of the room, rather than in the middle of the room. If people are facing the wall rather than the center of a room, the actor is less accessible to others. He is less available to exchange glances with anyone. This maximizes his privacy. The compartmentalization and enclosure of stalls also serves to maximize privacy.

We have examined one form of theory creation, where hypotheses came from observation. Hypotheses can be created by any form of social research. Hypotheses can be created from survey research, whether it be conducted with questionnaires or interviews, from highly structured laboratory experiments, from loosely structured field work, or from document analysis.

Hypotheses can be created purposefully or accidentally. One can conduct research with the objective of creating hypotheses about a particular behavioral phenomenon or social setting. Or one may come upon new hypotheses quite accidentally. In testing hypotheses, one frequently encounters unexpected research findings which can lead to a new hypothesis. The fact is that hypotheses come out of social research.

CREATING THEORY WITH SURVEY RESEARCH

Survey research is the most widely used research design in sociology. It involves constructing a research instrument, usually a questionnaire or interview schedule, which is then administered to respondents.

Survey research is an extremely flexible, versatile research design. It can be used to study a large or small sample of people. It is usually used with large samples, particularly when questionnaires are used. It can be used to study one group of respondents at one point in time or it can be used longitudinally. Survey research can focus on the effects on human group life of social variables such as age, sex, social class, race , or religion, or it can focus on more in-depth analyses of attitudes, feelings, and the subjective states of mind of respondents. It is usually used for the analysis of social variables. It can be used to create or to test hypotheses.

As its name implies, survey research involves surveying respondents in a community or group to obtain needed data. The data is given directly to the researcher by some willing respondent.

Of all research designs, survey research most clearly requires active, willful, mutual involvement of a researcher and respondent in the data collection process. Without this mutual participation, survey research would not be possible. The two major research instruments used in survey research are *questionnaires* and *interviews*. A *questionnaire* is composed of a series of written questions which are given directly to respondents for them to answer. The fact that these questions are written on paper and are read by the respondnent himself is important, as this distinguishes questionnaires from interviews. Respondents answering questionnaires read the written questions themselves.

In *interviews*, questions are read to respondents by interviewers. If questions are read aloud to respondents by an interviewer, the written document which contains the questions is called an interview schedule and not a questionnaire.

An exercise which I have used to show my students how hypotheses and theories are created with survey research involves their seeking social determinants of good grades in school. The *concepts* which students most frequently cite as probably affecting the kinds of grades students earn include age, marital status, living conditions, and outside employment. The class constructs an exploratory interview schedule which is designed to assess whether or not age, marital status, living conditions or outside employment do affect or are related to grades in school. This research is exploratory inasuch as no hypothesis is being tested. A possible relation between concepts is being explored. If relationships between some of these concepts are found to exist, hypotheses can be created reflecting the nature of the relationship that is found.

The implicit assumption of the exploratory research is that age, marital status, and outside work are factors which do affect grades. The variables of these concepts are treated as independent variables, occurring in time before grades are earned. These factors are seen as directly influencing the value of one's grades. This assumption must be empirically validated; that is, we must statistically prove that what we assume are legitimate independent variables are in fact independent variables affecting the dependent variables high or low grades.

SAMPLING: Before constructing a research instrument, one must clearly define the population from which a sample is to be drawn. The nature of the people to whom the questionnaire or interview schedule will be administered can affect the wording and structure of items in the instrument.

A *population* is a group of people or objects sharing some definable, measureable characteristic. In this class assignment, the population consisted of undergraduate students enrolled at a particular college.

A *sample* consists of some part of a defined population. A sample always includes less than the sum of all persons or objects within a population. If we were interested in studying a population which contained few members. we might not have to choose a sample from that population. We could survey the entire population. If we were interested in studying the relation of age to grades among students living in a given cooperative housing unit, and this entire population included thirty people, we could survey all thirty students. If all thirty students completed our research instrument, we could say that the study was done with an entire population. If, however, all but one of the thirty students completed the research instrument, the research would have been conducted with a sample, not the population. By definition, if not every member of a population is included in the research findings, then one has a sample from the population, not the entire population.

The purpose of sampling is to obtain from a population a manageable and yet meaningful number of responents for one's research. To be manageable, the sample must be small enough so that the study is conducted within the limits of time, money and manpower resources. To be meaningful, the sample must be large enough so that respondents can be segmented into a number of analytic categories. When this is done, enough respondents must occupy each category to make statistically meaningful interpretations of data. Where there is a sample of 50 persons, the number of respondents in each cell of a simple four-fold table becomes very small, even where the respondents are divided equally.

Where there are twelve or thirteen respondents in a cell, the effect of error becomes very great. One mistake in coding or recording an answer could have a significant effect on the overall interpretation of the table.

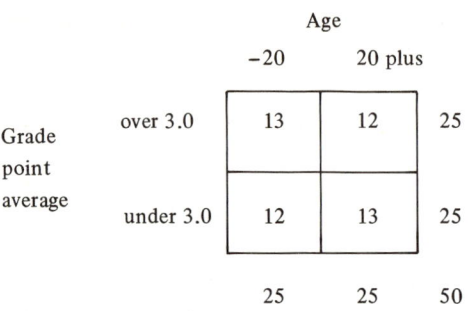

Figure 2.2. Grade point average of students by age.

To allow for analytic flexibility and meaningful statistical interpretation of data obtained in survey research, samples are usually kept as large as possible within the limits of one's resources.

There are basically two types of samples used in sociology: nonprobability samples and probability samples. A *non-probability* sample exists when the sampling procedure affords no way of ascertaining the probability that any one member of a population will be selected for a sample. In many non-probability samples, there is no assurance that every person in a population has some chance of being included in a sample. Non-probability samples are often used in sociology because the sampling procedures are much less costly and are easier to implement than are probability sampling techniques.

Probability sampling is characterized by the facts that, 1) there is a calculable probability for each member of the population that he will be included in a sample, and 2) for every member of a population, his chances of being included in a sample are greater than zero. In simple random sampling each person in a defined population has the same chance of being included in a sample and this chance is greater than zero.

In constructing a sample from which we would examine the social determinants of grades, a modified accidental sampling technique was used. Accidental sampling is a form of non-probability sampling. It is done by taking respondents as they happen to come along; there is no systematic sampling procedure. The inquiring photographer who asks people questions as they happen to pass by and the marketing researcher who polls the opinions of shoppers in grocery stores are examples of researchers using accidental sampling.

The sampling technique used in our exploratory research was a modified accidental sampling because, though students were asked to select any six persons who were undergraduates attending the school, they were also asked to try to get diversity in the age of their respondents. They were asked to avoid getting respondents that were either all old or all young. In this sense, the sample was guided by a sampling criterion and was not purely accidental. A sample of 61 persons was obtained from the population "undergraduate students attending X College." Once the population to be sampled is known, the research instrument can be constructed.

THE RESEARCH INSTRUMENT: In constructing the interview schedule, the distinction made in Chapter I between concepts and variables becomes crucial. "Age" is a concept. "Grades in school" is a concept.

In measuring how age affects grades in school, we must devise variables for these concepts. Variables, remember, are dimensions, categories, or values of a concept. In measuring the age of college students, we can ask the question "How old are you?" The alternatives we supply for recording the answers are a reflection of how many variables of the concept we are willing to take into account. We can create a question that will provide eleven variables of the concept age:

How old are you?
____under 17   ____21
____17   ____22
____18   ____23
____19   ____24
____20   ____25
                    ____over 25

We can create a question which takes into account four variables of age:

How old are you?
____under 17
____17-19
____20-22
____Over 22

We can create a question which takes into account only two variables of age.

           ____19 and under
           ____over 19

The decision about how many variables of a concept one will take into account is called *coding*. Coding involves placing all the alternatives of response to a question into a given number of categories or dimensions. Each dimension constitutes a variable of the concept being measured.*

The number of variables that are taken into account and the kind of variables taken into account will greatly affect the wording of hypotheses derived from research.

If only two variables of age are taken into account, as in the last example, the hypothesis that we could derive from this is that students aged 19 and under get (higher or lower) grades than do students over 19 years of age. If, however, three or more variables of age were coded, and if for each older age category grades were higher, we could derive a hypothesis that, "among college students, age will be positively related to grades in school"; or "the older a group of students is, the higher will be their grades." This is a higher level hypothesis than one could derive from an examination of only two age variables. The addition of the third variable makes the higher level hypothesis possible.

Coding can be done before or after a research instrument is administered. If variables are established prior to the administration of a question, the question is said to be *pre-coded*. Pre-coded questions are somtimes called multiple choice questions or forced choice questions. In the examples just cited, the questions consisting of eleven, four, and two age variables constitute pre-coded, closed-ended questions.

Sometimes researchers will not want to code responses to a question until after they can see a frequency distribution of responses to the question. For statistical flexibility, it is convenient to have responses divided into many categories rather than having most responses in one category. If we want to know the effect of age on getting good grades, we cannot learn much if the vast majority of respondents are all in the same age category. We risk this if we pre-code the alternatives into categories which are very broad. If we sampled college undergraduates and pre-coded responses into age categories of 17-21, 22-25, and over 25, the vast majority of our respondents would probably fall in the 17-21 category.

To insure that respondents are divided into several different age categories, two different measures of age could be taken. The respondent could be given a closed-ended question with many variables. After a frequency distribution of the responses was taken, several categories could then be combined. This would reduce the number of variables for the analysis of data but would ensure that responses were distributed over several age categories.

In creating a theory of grades, we will use the approach and the data used in one of my recent introductory sociology classes. These students initially measured age by using eleven age variables in their interview schedule. The class got the following frequency distribution of responses:

Age	Number of respondents
under 17	0
17	0
18	8
19	15
20	13
21	10
22	4
23	2
24	1
25	2
over 25	6

Figure 2.3. Frequency distribution of students by age.

They reduced the eleven variables to three. They combined respondents who were 18 and 19 years of age into one variable, combined 20, 21 and 22 year old respondents into another variable, and combined all persons 23 years old and older into a third variable. The new frequency distribution, with the three variables looked as follows:

18-19	23
20-22	27
23 and over	11

The number of categories used to dimensionalize a concept can always be reduced but can never be increased after a question is administered.

An alternative approach to delaying a final coding would have been to ask respondents how old they were, leaving the answer *open-ended*. In open-ended questions, the respondent is left a blank space to answer a question in his own words. An open-ended question seeking a respondents' age might look as follows:

How old are you? _____

Once a frequency distribution of the open-ended responses is constructed, the responses can be coded into a number of variables. Where quantitative data is sought, the difference between open-ended and closed-ended questions becomes a difference when concepts are coded into variables. Closed-ended questions are pre-coded. Answers are placed in categories before the respondent gets the research instrument. Open-ended questions are coded into categories after respondents complete the research instrument.

Open-ended questions are usually not used to measure easily quantifiable concepts such as age. They are usually used to give respondents freedom to express their feelings, perceptions and opinions in their own words. They are good for measuring the subjective states of minds of respondents. They give the researcher confidence that he is measuring the precise feelings of respondents without structuring these feelings with analytic categories. But open-ended questions also have some disadvantages. Not everyone will perceive the demands of the question in the same way or answer the question in the same terms. Some respondents may answer in terms of how many years, months, days and hours old they are. Others may write avoidance answers such as "Old enough to know better". Closed-ended questions, on the other hand, insure a standardized form of answer and further help respondents comprehend what is asked for in a question. Furthermore, where closed-ended questions are used, ambiguities are reduced for the researcher in interpreting the meaning of an answer. There can be no doubt about the meaning of an "X" on a given line. There are sometimes problems in interpreting the meaning of answers to open-ended questions.

SCALES : Coding is usually done by placing variables in a nominal, ordinal or interval scale. Nominal scales consist of at least two named categories by which respondents can be categorized. Categorizing religions as Catholic, Protestant, Jewish and other; categorizing nationalities as Irish, Italian, Greek, French, etc.; categorizing political party affiliation as Republican, Democrat, Socialist, other; or categorizing sex as male and female, are all examples of coding using variables which form nominal scales. Nominal scales are non-mathematical; we get no notion of which category in a nominal scale is "more than" or "less than" any other catgory. We get no mathematical equivalence for categories in a nominal scale. Yet nominal scales are considered to be scales inasmuch as all categories within the scale have a logical relationship to one another; the categories are all religions, nationalities, political parties and so forth.

Ordinal scales allow the researcher to assess whether some respondents have more, the same amount or less of one concept than other respondents. Ordinal scales are not precise enough, however, to assess exactly how much more or less of one concept some respondents have than others. If we ask respondents whether they strongly agree, agree, disagree, or strongly disagree with a statement, we have established responses in an ordinal scale.

Interval scales include the notion of greater, the same as, or less than and also enable the researcher to make precise mathematical assessments of how much more or less apart respondents are along a dimension. To achieve this, variables must have an exact numerical value. In interval scales, the difference between categories can be precisely ascertained; the values between categories on the scale are usually constant and equal. A thermometer is a good example of an interval scale, where each line signifies a tenth of a degree.

VALIDITY: A research instrument is said to be valid if it measures what the researcher intends it should measure. The assessment of validity is highly complex because there are many different ways in which measures can fail to be valid. There is no one way to assess the validity of a measurement; different techniques of assessing validity tap specific sources of error, but no one techique assesses all possible sources of error.

One source of error occurs where questions are so vague that respondents can interpret them in different ways and answer them along dimensions which are incomparable. If we asked an open-ended question such as, "What is your class standing?", some respondents might respond along the dimension Freshman, Sophomore, Junior, Senior and others might put 123 or some other number, signifying their rank by grade point average in their graduating class. Furthermore, we have no way of assessing, for the students responding Freshman, Sophomore, Junior and Senior, whether they are using number of units completed or number of years attending the school as a criterion for their answers. These are problems which affect the internal validity of such a question.

This kind of validity error can be detected through pre-testing the research instrument. Pretesting involves administering the research instrument to a small independent sample of persons before administering the instrument to the main sample. The pre-test sample constitutes a kind of mini-sample composed of persons with the same characteristics as will be manifest in the main sample.

The pre-test sample must be independent from the main sample. Nobody can be in both samples; a person who is in the pre-test sample should be excluded from the main sample. If the pre-test sample and the main sample are not kept discrete, it would mean that for some questions on the final research instrument, some respondents will be answering the question for the first time, never having seen the question before, and those who participated in the pre-test may be answering questions which they have seen before. This introduces a potential source of bias to the research.

The pre-test is a replica of the intended testing procedure. Everything is done exactly as it will be done under actual test conditions. This gives the test instrument a realistic trial. It further gives interviewers a chance to practice their procedures, to polish up their approach and iron out any difficulties which would later cause mistakes in concrete research results. Pre-testing also gives the researcher some insight as to what he can expect in terms of research results, as even the data analysis part of the research procedure is conducted in the pre-test.

As a result of the pre-test, questions are reworded to make them more precise and straightforward; answers are recoded into categories which are perhaps more meaningful to respondents or more useful in analysis to the researcher; questions are added to the research instrument to cover previously unexplored areas which were discovered in the pre-test process; and questions are omitted which have proven less productive than anticipated. Although pre-testing can be expensive and time-consuming, it often enhances the validity of a study.

A second source of validity error is linked to the time at which a study is conducted and the conditions under which it is conducted. If we are interested in assessing a student's grade point average for a given semester, we could not ask him about his grades until after his final grades were given. If we asked a student what he thought his grade point average would be at the end of the semester, based on his current performance in classes, we would not be measuring his actual grade point average but would be measuring his expectation for grades or, perhaps his wishful thinking.

Another source of validity error occurs where empirical indicators of terms do not mirror the definition of those terms. If we come to define "grade point average" as a student's cumulative grade point average for all courses taken in his college career, we cannot measure grade point average by asking students for the grade point average they obtained in their last semester. In doing this, we would in fact be measuring one type of grade point average when we intended to measure another. This is a validity error inasmuch as we would not be measuring what we thought we were measuring or intended to measure.

One might well wonder if any study can ever escape errors of validity. They can come from so many sources that the researcher has difficulty recognizing them, not to mention correcting them. One never knows of factors which reduce validity in a study until somebody discovers them and points them out. It is probably safe to say that all social research contains errors which reduce validity. In all studies the researcher is either testing things of which he is unaware or is not measuring what he thinks he is measuring. Social scientist simply do not have the controls to eliminate such errors and, even if they did, the highly controlled nature of the research would probably constitute a validity error in and of itself. The objective, then, is to reduce validity errors as much as possible, and forget about eliminating them altogether.

RELIABILITY : A measurement instrument, whether it be one question or an integrated test of several hundred questions, is said to have reliability if it measures phenomena *consistently* over time. A measurement instrument is reliable if it is relatively immune to variations in testing conditions. One technique which is frequently used to assess the reliability of an instrument over time is the test-retest technique. Here an index measuring what is normally a fairly stable phenomenon, such as self-image or socio-economic class, is administered to respondents at one point in time. It is then administered to the same respondents at a later point in time and the results are compared for their consistency. If the results are unstable for the group tested, it can be inferred that the research instrument is too susceptible to external variation and therefore lacks reliability. Tests which assess the degree to which an instrument yields consistent results under differential external conditions are said to measure the instrument's *external reliability*.

When there is a series of several questions, all tapping a single concept such as self-image or socio-economic status, another factor of reliability becomes important, internal consistency. Where there are multiple indices of a single concept, these indices should be interchangeable. Further, any subsegment of the whole should reveal the same findings as the entire instrument. If an instrument has internal consistency (internal reliability), one should be able to change the order of questions, or omit some questions, without seriously affecting the overall results.

One way to test the internal reliability of a series of indices which measure the same concept is called a split-half reliability test. This involves taking items tapping the same concept and dividing them in half. If we are trying to measure whether a person has an overall positive or negative self image and have ten questions to assess what a person thinks of himself, we could divide these questions in half by making questions 1-5 and questions 6-10 the two halves; or we could take questions 1, 3, 5, 7 and 9 for one half and questions 2, 4, 6, 8, and 10 for the other; or we could select the halves randomly by drawing numbers from a hat. One checks split-half reliability by comparing the results obtained in the two halves. If the results are similar (we would not expect them to be identical), this indicates internal reliability of the whole measure.

Another way in which internal reliability can be assessed is through a technique called item analysis. This involves individually analyzing each item or question to check its consistency with the whole measurement instrument of which it is a part.

In analyzing reliability, it is crucial to compare questions which have the same intended objective, which attempt to measure the same phenomenon. If a test measures self-image and the test is divided into sub-tests, some measuring sense of political efficacy, some measuring vocational satisfaction, some measuring assessments of physical characteristics, some measuring attitudinal predispositions, we would expect the reliability within each sub-test to be much stronger than the reliability between sub-tests, because they are measuring different phenomenon. Yet they do have a common bond, and so we expect that there will be some internal consistency between measures. The expectations we impose in assessing reliability must be flexible, to meet the realities of the instrument we evaluate.

Reliability and validity are inter-related: *If a test is not reliable it will not be valid either.* If a test does not measure consistently then we never know at any point in time what it is measuring, which means by definition that the measure is not valid.

The reverse of this is not necessarily true, however. A measurement can be invalid, that is, not measure what the researcher thinks it measures, and measure this thing very consistently. It would then lack validity but still be reliable.

Errors of validity and reliability seriously impede the utility of social research. Economically, it is much wiser to build into a research design, safeguards to protect against validity and reliability errors rather than to expend the time, money and energy on a study and then in the end find it worthless because these errors were undetected. There is a greet need for more easy, economical techniques for the detection of these errors in social research.

CREATING HYPOTHESES: When surveying the effects of age on students' grades we compared the grade point averages of groups of students. The grade point average of 18-19 year olds were compared to the grade point average of 20-22 year olds and so on for all variables of age.

To do this we needed a measure which allowed us to summarize the grades of a *group* of students and which allowed us to compare the collective grades of one group to the collective grades of another group of students. Three such measures are *mean*, *median*, and *mode*. All three are measures of central tendency in a frequency distribution.

Before describing how mean, median and mode can be used to compare the grades of different aged students, it would be best to construct a frequency distribution of single semester grade point averages for students in the three age groups.

A frequency distribution is a convenient vehicle for organizing data. A frequency distribution reveals the total variety of values a variable obtains when a research question is asked. It records the frequency (the number of times) each variable was given as a response. The frequency distribution in Figure 2.4 lists the grade point averages students said they received in their previous semester of school and records how many students—in each of the three age categories—said they received this grade point average.

The axis at the left-hand margin lists grade point averages (rounded off to the nearest tenth) that could be given as responses by students. The first column records the number of respondents aged 18 and 19, who stated they obtained a given grade point average in their previous semester's work. The second column records the number of respondents,

54   *Theory and Measurement in Sociology*

aged 20-22, who stated they obtained a given grade point average in the previous semester. The third column records the number of respondents, aged 23 and over, who stated they obtained a given grade point average in the previous semester.

Age of Undergraduate Students

Grade Point Averages	18-19	20-22	23 and older
4.0			
3.9			
3.8			1
3.7		2	
3.6		1	1
3.5	3	1	1
3.4	1	2	1
3.3		2	1
3.2	3	5	2
3.1	1	1	
3.0	6	6	2
2.9			
2.8	1	2	1
2.7	2	1	
2.6			
2.5	3	3	1
2.4			
2.3		1	
2.2			
2.1			
2.0			
below 2.0			

Figure 2.4. Frequency distribution of students obtaining a given grade point average, by age.

We can assess the relationship between age and grades by comparing the mean grade point averages of each age group. If the mean grade point average of each succesively older group is higher, then this would support a hypothesis that there is a direct relationship between age and grades in college. *A mean is the same as an average.* Means are most easily computed from a frequency distribution. The frequency distribution of grades for 18 and 19 year old undergraduates is reproduced in Figure 2.5.

Values of X (grades) X	The Frequency of X f_X	The sum of X ΣX
3.5	3	10.50
3.4	1	3.4
3.2	3	9.6
3.1	1	3.1
3.0	6	18.0
2.8	1	2.8
2.7	2	5.4
2.5	3	7.5
2.0	3	6.0
	$f_X = N = 23$	$\Sigma X = 66.3$

Figure 2.5. Frequency distribution of grade point averages obtained by students aged 18 and 19.

The first column (signified by X) represents all values of grades obtained by these respondents. The second column (f_x) tells us how many respondents, aged 18 and 19, state they had the grade point average reflected in the first column (rows run horizontally across the page, columns run vertically up and down). The sum of the frequencies in the f_x column is N, the total number of respondents aged 18 and 19. Each value in the third column is the *sum* of a particular value of X, which is obtained by multiplying the values of X (the grade point average) by the frequency that value of X is obtained. By adding the figures in the third column, we obtain the sum of all Xs, the sum of all the grade point averages obtained by our 18 and 19 year old respondents. The formula for computing a mean is

$$\overline{X} = \frac{\Sigma X}{N}$$

The mean is the sum of all values of X obtained (the sum of column three) divided by the total number of respondents from which values of X were obtained (the sum of column two). The mean grade point average of the 18-19 year old undergraduates sampled is 2.88.

$$\overline{X} = \frac{\Sigma X}{N} = \frac{66.3}{23} = 2.88$$

Rather than outlining the steps for computing the mean grade point average of the 20-22 year old group and the 23 year olds and over group, the reader is encouraged to complete a full frequency distribution for these groups based on the data supplied on page 74. If the computation is done accurately, the 20-22 year olds should be found to have a mean grade point average of 3.07. The 23 and over group exhibits a mean grade point average of 3.20. Age is found to be positively or directly related to grades as measured by mean grade point averages.

Where samples are small, means are greatly affected by deviant, extreme cases. In cases where an unusually high or unusually low score is apt to greatly affect a mean, it is often advisable to use another measure of central tendency, such as median or mode.

The median designates the "middle score" within an array of scores. Medians are relatively uncomplicated where there is an odd number of scores in an array. The scores are arranged in ascending order and the middle score is obtained by counting inward from both ends of the array.

Where there is an even number of scores in an array, there will be two middle scores. The average of these two middle scores is the median score.

Using the frequency distributions used to compute the mean grade point average of our three age groups, we find that the median grade point average for 18 and 19 year olds is 3.0. The median grade point average for 20-22 year olds is 3.1. The median grade point average for 23 year olds and above is 3.2. There is thus a direct relationship between age of students and their grades whether mean or median grade point average is used as a measure of grades obtained by each age group.

A third measure of central tendency in a frequency distribution is the *mode. Mode signifies the score having the highest frequency in an array.* This measure is particularly useful where scores are narrowly dispersed (where they exhibit a narrow range) around the mode. The scores which we obtained do not exhibit such a narrow range. If there are two responses which have the same frequency and if this frequency is the highest obtained for any response in the distribution, we say that there are two modes and describe the sample as having a bi-modal distribution.

The most frequently obtained grade point average among the 18-19 year olds was 3.0, with six respondents giving that response. The modal grade point average of the 18-19 year olds was 3.0. Likewise, the modal grade point average among 20-22 year olds was 3.0. The oldest age group exhibits a bi-modal distribution with two modes being 3.0 and 3.2.

It is much more difficult to create a hypothesis linking age and grades from an analysis of modes. No consistent trend is evident. As the nature of the distribution of grades does not really justify the use of mode as a measure of central tendency in these three frequency distributions, and as the analysis of modal frequencies does not run contrary to what was found in our comparisons of mean and median grade point averages, the hypothesis that the older the students are, the higher will be their grades was adopted.

The Analysis of Variance: Means, medians and modes do not convey information about the variability or dispersion of scores. Frequency distributions do convey this information, but not in an easily digested, easily interpreted form. Two measures which are used in sociology to convey the variability of scores about a measure of central tendency are *mean deviation* and *standard deviation*. We will briefly examine these measures using our frequency distribution of grades.

Both the mean deviation and the standard deviation can be used to measure the dispersion of scores about the mean, median or mode of a distribution. As mean is the most appropriate measure of central tendency in most cases, we will compute the mean deviation and standard deviation of scores around the mean in our examples.

In computing the deviation of scores around a mean, if we simply summed the deviations from the mean the result would always be zero because the positive and negative deviations from the mean would always cancel each other out. To obtain a measure of variance, then, we ignore postive and negative signs and compute the absolute variations from the mean. This is what is done when mean deviation is computed. One can eliminate positive and negative signs by squaring variations from a mean, and this technique is used when standard deviations are computed.

The mean deviation is a measure summarizing the average dispersion of all combined scores from an arithmetic mean. In general, a low figure will indicate little dispersion, that is, scores will not range very far from the mean. A high figure indicates great variability with scores ranging far from the mean. Where there is a small sample, the mean deviation score is severely affected by deviant cases. The meaningfulness of this measure is enhanced by large samples.

The formula for computing the mean deviaton is:

$$\text{mean deviation} = \frac{\sum f|X - \overline{X}|}{N}$$

The mean deviation is obtained by subtracting each raw score (X) from the mean ($\overline{X}$). This difference is multiplied by the frequency with which that score appeared. These products for each value of X, are added, and this sum is divided by the total number of scores in the sample. Using a frequency distribution of grade point averages obtained by undergraduate students, aged 18-19, 20-22 and 23 and over, we can illustrate how a mean deviation is computed.

X	$|X - \overline{X}|$	f(X)	$f|X - \overline{X}|$
3.5	.62	3	1.86
3.4	.52	1	.52
3.2	.32	3	.96
3.1	.22	1	.22
3.0	.12	6	.72
2.8	.08	1	.08
2.7	.18	2	.36
2.5	.38	3	1.14
		20 = N	5.86 = $\Sigma f X - \overline{X}$

Figure 2.6. Frequency distribution of grade point averages for students aged 18-19.

The mean grade point average in this distribution is 2.88. The highest grade point average obtained (3.5) is .62 grade points higher than the mean of the distibution, therefore $|X - \overline{X}|$ for 3.5 is .62 (3.5-2.88=.62).

In computing the mean deviation of grades in this frequency distribution we follow the formula as follows:

$$\frac{\Sigma f|X - X|}{N} = \frac{5.86}{20} = .293$$

This means that an average dispersion from the mean in this frequency distribution is a very low .293 of a grade point. This is a very minimal dispersion, particularly considering the small size of the sample, where one very deviant case would have significantly increased the mean deviation. This minimal dispersion could have been anticipated by looking at the range of scores in the distribution. *The range of scores in a distribution is the span which exists between the highest and lowest scores in the distribution.* The range of scores in Figure 2.6 covers only 1.0 grade points, the grades ranging from 3.5 to 2.5. This is a narrow range considering that the range theoretically could have been 4 grade points, from 0 to 4.0.

X	X - X̄	(f)	f X - X̄
3.7	.63	2	1.26
3.6	.53	1	.53
3.5	.43	1	.43
3.4	.33	2	.66
3.3	.23	2	.46
3.2	.13	5	.65
3.1	.03	1	.03
3.0	.07	6	.42
2.8	.27	2	.54
2.7	.37	1	.37
2.5	.57	3	1.71
2.3	.77	1	.77
		27 = N	7.83 = f X - X̄

Figure 2.7. Frequency distribution of grade point average for undergraduate students aged 20-22.

The frequency distribution of grade point averages for undergraduates aged 20-22 is presented in Figure 2.7.

The mean grade point average in this distribution is 3.07. We compute the mean deviation of grades in this distribution as follows:

$$\frac{\sum f|X - \bar{X}|}{N} = \frac{7.83}{27} = 2.90$$

Despite the fact that the range of grade point averages is slightly wider than in the distribution for 18-19 year olds (1.4 vs. 1.0) the mean deviation of grades in this distribution is slightly less (.290). Both distributions thus far exhibit very little variation of grades from the mean. The mean deviation in both distributions is almost identical (.293 vs. .290).

The frequency distribution of grade point averages for undergraduate students aged 23 and over is presented in Figure 2.8.

The mean grade point average in this distibution is 3.20. The mean deviation of scores within the distribution is computed as follows:

$$\frac{fX - \bar{X}}{N} = \frac{3.10}{11} = .282$$

This distribution has the lowest average dispersion of scores from the arithmetic mean, yet it is not very much lower than the mean deviation of either of the other distributions.

X	X - X̄	(f)	f X - X̄
3.8	.60	1	.60
3.6	.40	1	.40
3.5	.30	1	.30
3.4	.20	1	.20
3.3	.10	1	.10
3.2	0	2	
3.0	.20	2	.40
2.8	.40	1	.40
2.5	.70	1	.70
		11 = N	3.10 = Σf|X - X̄|

Figure 2.8. Frequency distribution of grade point averages for undergraduate students aged 23 and over.

Once the mean deviation of a distribution is obtained, it must then be interpreted. This is characteristic of all statistical computations. Statistics never interpret themselves. A computation is made and then the researcher must evaluate and make sense of it.

A mean deviation of .282, .290 or .293 grade poin.s in a distribution of grade point averages could be interpreted as constituting a large or a small deviation from the mean. Given the fact that we had three small samples and that deviant cases, particularly in a small sample, will severely increase the mean deviation, and given the fact that the possible range of grade point averages was four points, we interpret these mean deviations as reflecting a narrow dispersion around the mean. Just how large a mean dispersion we would be willing to tolerate and still consider the dispersion to be narrow is a tough judgmental question. Taking into account the size of the sample, the kind of sampling that was done, and the purpose of measurement, the researcher would have to establish boundaies which would enable him to interpret his measurement as constituting a wide or narrow dispersion around a mean.

STANDARD DEVIATION: Another dispersion around a mean is the standard deviation. The formula for finding the standard deviation is:

$$\sigma = \sqrt{\frac{\Sigma (X - \bar{X})^2}{N}}$$

To compute the standard deviation of a distribution, we subtract each score obtained (X) from the mean of the distribution ($\bar{X}$), square each

Measurement and Theory Creation 61

X	$(X - \bar{X})$	$(X - \bar{X})^2$	f(X)	$f(X - \bar{X})^2$
3.5	.62	.3844	3	1.1532
3.4	.52	.2704	1	.2704
3.2	.32	.1024	3	.3072
3.1	.22	.0484	1	.0484
3.0	.12	.0144	6	.0864
2.8	.08	.0064	1	.0064
2.7	.18	.0324	2	.0648
2.5	.38	.1444	3	.4332
			N = 20	$\Sigma(X-\bar{X})^2$ = 2.3700

Figure 2.9. Frequency distribution for the computation of the standard deviation of grade point averages from the mean for undergraduate students aged 18-19.

difference, add all the squared differences for each value of X, divide this sum by the total number of respondents, and compute the square root of this quotient.

Using the frequency distribution of grade point averages for students aged 18-19, we can compute the standard deviation of this distribution as shown in Figure 2.9.

$$\sigma = \sqrt{\frac{(x - \bar{X})^2}{N}} = \sqrt{\frac{2.3700}{20}} = \sqrt{.1185} = .3442$$

X	$(X - \bar{X})$	$(X - \bar{X})^2$	f(X)	$f(X - \bar{X})^2$
3.7	.63	.3969	2	.7938
3.6	.53	.2809	1	.2809
3.5	.43	.1849	1	.1849
3.4	.33	.1089	2	.2178
3.3	.23	.0529	2	.1058
3.2	.13	.0169	5	.0845
3.1	.03	.0009	1	.0009
3.0	.07	.0049	6	.0294
2.8	.27	.0729	2	.1458
2.7	.37	.1369	1	.1369
2.5	.57	.3249	3	.9747
2.3	.77	.5929	1	.5929
			N = 27	$\Sigma(X - \bar{X})^2$ = 3.5483

Figure 2.10. Frequency distribution for the computation of the standard deviation of grade point averages from the mean for undergraduate students aged 20-22.

The standard deviation of grade point averages from the mean in the distribution for 20-22 year old students was computed as shown in Figure 2.10.

$$\sigma = \sqrt{\frac{(X - \bar{X})^2}{N}} = \sqrt{\frac{3.5483}{27}} = \sqrt{.1314} = .3624$$

The computation of the standard deviation of grade point averages from the mean in the distribution for students 23 years and older is shown in Figure 2.11.

X	$(X - \bar{X})$	$(X - \bar{X})^2$	f(X)	$f(X - \bar{X})^2$
3.8	.60	.3600	1	.3600
3.6	.40	.1600	1	.1600
3.5	.30	.0900	1	.0900
3.4	.20	.0400	1	.0400
3.3	.10	.0100	1	.0100
3.2	0	0	2	.0000
3.0	.20	.0400	2	.0800
2.8	.40	.1600	1	.1600
2.5	.70	.4900	1	.4900
			N = 11	$\Sigma(X - \bar{X})^2 = 1.3900$

Figure 2.11. Frequency distribution for the computation of the standard deviation of grade point averages from the mean for undergraduate students aged 23 and older.

$$\sigma = \sqrt{\frac{(X - \bar{X})^2}{N}} = \sqrt{\frac{1.39}{11}} = \sqrt{.1263} = .3553$$

The computation of standard deviations indicated that the three age groups differed little in the extent to which their grades vary around the mean. All three groups exhibit grades with relatively little variance, a finding consistent with what we found when we computed the mean deviations of these distributions.

In order to fully understand the significance of these standard deviation scores, it is important to know the relevance of standard deviation to distributions which approximate normal curves. A normal curve is a symmetrical bell-shaped curve where the majority of cases fall near the mean and the frequency of scores descends as the scores get further and further from the mean score. A normal curve would look roughly like the curve in Figure 2.12.

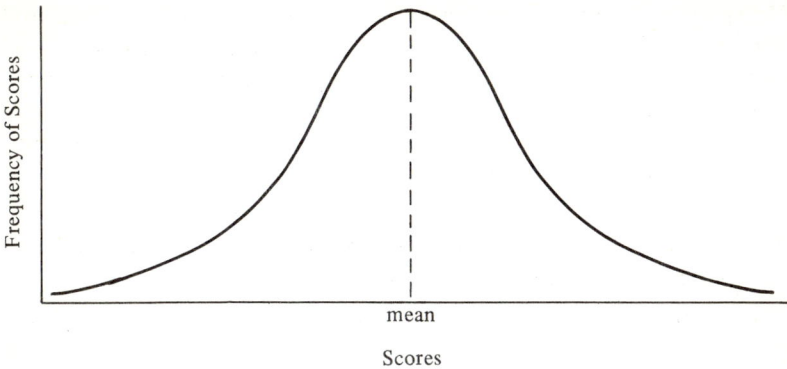

Figure 2.12. A normal curve.

Where scores and their frequencies are plotted on a curve and this curve approximates a normal curve, approximately 68.2% of the scores will fall within one standard deviation on both sides of the mean. Approximately 95.45% of the scores will fall within 2 standard deviations of the mean, and 99.73% of the scores will fall within 3 standard deviations of the mean. Our sample is just too small for the scores to approximate a normal curve. If the scores did approximate a normal curve, however, among 18-19 year olds, approximately 68.2% of the scores would fall between grade point averages of 2.5358 and 3.2242 (mean 2.88 plus and minus .3442, the standard deviation).

CREATING A THEORY OF GRADES: Thus far, our data justifies the hypothesis that the older students are, the higher will be their grades. In addition to being categorized by age, students were also divided into two groups according to their marital status. The empirical indictator for marital status was the question: "What was your marital status last semester?" Students were instructed to code a respondent as "married" if he was married at any time during the semester. This covered the contingencies of students marrying or divorcing during the semester. The mean grade point average of the married students was significantly higher than the mean grade point average of the unmarried students. Grade point average again was defined as the grade point average of a student over the previous semester only. Our findings led us to formulate a second hypothesis, namely that married students will get higher grades than will unmarried students.

Thinking that there would be a strong relation between age and marital status, a table was constructed relating these concepts and it was found that the older students are more likely to be married than are the younger students. In these findings, we can create three hypotheses which would constitute a theory of academic performance. The third hypothesis is derived from the first two.

1) The older students are, the higher will be their grades.
2) Married students will get higher grades than will unmarried students.
3) The older students are, the more likely that they will be married.

If we construct a matrix of these concepts, we know that our three hypotheses are required to inter-relate all concepts in the theory to each other to insure a logically complete theory.

	Age	Marital Status	Grades
Age		1	2
Marital Status			3
Grades			

Figure 2.13. Matrix of concepts in a theory of student grades.

One hypothesis must inter-relate age and marital status, which is done in hypothesis 3. Another hypothesis must inter-relate age and grades, which is done in hypothesis 1. One hypothesis must inter-relate marital status and grades, which is done in hypothesis 2. The theory is logically complete.

As theories consist of both hypotheses and definitions, all terms within the theory must be defined. Grades were defined as a student's grade point average for all grades received during the past semester. Married students were defined as any student who was married during any part of the previous semester. Older students were defined as students whose chronological age was higher than other students.

In constructing the theory of grades, we analyzed other concepts besides age, marital status, and grades. Upon examining the relation between work and grades, it was found that those who worked, in addition to attending school, obtained exactly the same mean grade point average as those who did not work. Working, whether part-time or full-time, seemed to be unrelated to grades.

Given this finding, the only way work could be included in the theory as a concept, which would allow the theory to maintain internal consistency, would be if work was also found to be unrelated to age and marital status. In fact, this was the case. There was nearly zero association between work, and either age, marital status, or grades. If we chose to, then, we could have included the clause, "whether or not they worked" at the end of each hypothesis in the theory.

In examining the effects of living situation on grades no conclusion could be obtained from the data inasmuch as very few students sampled lived in on-compus dormitory facilities.

We have created a theory of academic performance from survey research. The hypotheses composing the theory were grounded in the empirical world. They must now be tested in a variety of different times and places. The theory as it exists is purely descriptive. In time, additional hypotheses might be added to the theory to account for the descriptive findings.

CHAPTER 3

EVALUATING SOCIOLOGICAL THEORY

In our introduction, we started with the contention that constructing theory about human group life and measuring human group life were not distinct, isolated enterprises, but were interrelated parts of a single scientific process. That point is reinforced when we analyze how theories are evaluated in sociology. It is crucial to know the component parts of theory if one is to understnad the rationale of the steps taken in evaluating theory.

Theories are not tested directly. The hypotheses of which theories are composed are tested, and the total theoretical structure is evaluated in light of the test results. One gains faith in the external validity of a theory if all the hypotheses within that theory are empirically validated consistently over time.

Hypotheses are composed of terms. Terms are labels for concepts. Only when terms are defined can appropriate empirical indicators be devised to measure these terms. The key to testing hypotheses lies in knowing how to measure all terms within that hypothesis.

The first and probably most crucial step in testing a hypothesis is to comprehend the meaning of that hypothesis. This is conveyed through the definitions of the terms within the hypothesis.

TERMS AND CONCEPTS: A single term in a hypothesis can signify a number of alternative concepts. Assume that we are interested in testing the hypothesis: "the higher a student's class standing, the higher will be his grades." There are three key terms in this hypothesis: "student," "class standing," and "grades." Each term can signify several different concepts. "Student" can mean any person who is matriculated in any public or private college or university or it can mean any person who is matriculated in any public or private college or university *and* who is taking a minimum of six units. These are two different concepts of the term "student".

The term "class standing" can signify the number of years a student has attended a college or university, or it can signify the number of academic units for which a student has been given credit toward a degree, or it can signify the hierarchical ranking of students in a given graduating class by their academic performance (grade point average). "Class standing" as a term, then, can also signify several concepts.

"Grades" can signify the grade point average a student obtained in the last semester or quarter he completed, or it can signify a student's cumulative grade point average in all academic work completed.

The terms used in a hypothesis can signify a variety of conceptualizations. *The meaning of any hypothesis is not contained in the terms of that hypothesis but in the concepts which those terms signify.* We can thus have two hypotheses which are identical in the terms they contain. If the terms signify different concepts, however, then they are different hypotheses, inasmuch as they have different meanings.

1) "The higher a student's class standing, the higher will be his grades."
2) "The higher a student's class standing, the higher will be his grades."

Though one's definition of the terms "student" and "grades" may be identical in these hypotheses, these are two different hypotheses if, in the first hypothesis, class standing is defined as "a hierarchical ranking of students by the number of academic units they are credited with toward their degree" and if in the second hypothesis we define class standing as "the hierarchical ranking of students within a graduating class by their academic performance (grade point average)." Though the two hypotheses have identical terms, they mean different things if the same term contained in both of them signify different concepts.

Because the meaning of a hypothesis is lodged in concepts, it is crucial, before one tests a hypothesis, that he define each term within the hypothesis. Only then does the researcher clearly articulate exactly what he is testing.

The fact that a single term can have different meanings presents a potential source of confusion and error for a researcher. In testing a hypothesis which has been created by someone else, the tester must define the concepts in that hypothesis exactly as the creator of the hypothesis defined them. This is the tester's only guarantee that he is in fact testing the same hypothesis that the creator devised. If he changes the definition of any concept within the creator's hypothesis, then he is testing a different hypothesis. If he alters the meaning of an original hypothesis and his research fails to validate that hypothesis, he may assert that the original hypothesis is invalid; this assertion, however, would be incorrect, inasmuch as he had never really tested the original but rather had tested a substitute hypothesis.

Research is said to have internal validity if a researcher measures what he thinks he is measuring. The validity of measurement in social research can be enhanced if all key terms within a hypothesis are clearly and explicitly defined before any effort is made to test that hypothesis.

The fact that the hypothesis tested is not always the hypothesis one intended to test is not always the fault of the researcher testing the hypothesis. Validity errors can stem from the fact that the researcher who created the hypothesis failed to explicitly define what he meant when he used a term. What enables a hypothesis to be empirically testable is that the exact meaning of that hypothesis is ascertainable. This can only occur if all terms contained in the hypothesis are defined.

AN EXAMPLE: In 1962, I was involved in a research project to test the hypothesis that, among rank-and-file voters, opinions held about controversial political issues would not be related to one's being a Democrat or Republican. The hypothesis was tested by interviewing 432 Berkeley, California voters less than two weeks before a state-wide election.

The hypothesis was derived from the research findings of Herbert McCloskey, et al.[8]

McCloskey compared Democratic and Republican party leaders with party rank-and-file voters regarding their views on controversial social and political issues. He found that Democratic leaders differed consistently from Republican leaders in their opinions on these issues, but that among rank-and-file voters, Democrats and Republicans differed very little in their opinions on the issues. In testing our hypothesis, there was no attempt to replicate the McCloskey study. We were merely attempting to test a hypothesis suggested by McCloskey's research.

In fact, McCloskey's research could not be replicated as he reported it, inasmuch as he gave no indication of how he defined or measured rank-and-file Democrats and Republicans. To replicate research, one

---

[8] Herbert McCloskey, Paul J. Hoffman, R. O'Hara, "Issue Conflict and Consensus Among Party Leaders and Followers." *American Political Science Review*, 54, June 1960. Pgs. 406-427.

must know how all concepts in an original hypothesis are defined and measured.

In testing our hypothesis, we had to define "rank-and-file voters," "opinions held about controversial political issues," and "Democrat or Republican." We defined rank-and-file voter in terms of a sampling procedure, namely, a rank and file voter was a person selected randomly from precinct lists of registered voters. In fact, with this procedure, we may have sampled some party leaders, as well as rank-and-file voters, but it was felt that this definition was precise enough for our purposes. McCloskey had the resources to obtain a national, cross-sectional sample. We only had resources to obtain samples from precincts. This affected conceptual definitions. "Party leaders" is defined by McCloskey, et al., as persons who attend a national party convention; and adopting this definition, we would have very few people in a precinct as party leaders. Given this fact, our definition seemed appropriate. The fact that our definition has us sampling from precinct lists of registered voters limits the population on which our hypothesis is to be tested; persons who were not registered voters were not tested.

We defined "opinions held about controversial political issues," as whether respondents agreed or disagreed with statements which were being heatedly debated by the politcal candidates running for office at that time. Six statements were presented to respondents:

1) The government should provide better medical care for older people.
2) Members of the Communist Party should not be allowed to speak on University and college campuses.
3) Capital punishment should be abolished.
4) Too much of the money spent on welfare in this state goes to people who don't really need it.
5) Our children would be better off if our schools went back to the three R's--reading, writing, and arithmetic.
6) I would favor strong American action to get rid of Castro.

Republican candidates were generally voicing agreement with statements 2, 4, 5, and 6 while Democratic candidates were generally voicing agreement with statements 1 and 3.

In defining Democrat and Republican, it was tempting to define a respondent's party affiliation as the party he claimed to be affiliated with when he registered to vote. Given this definition, all one would have to do to measure this concept is record whether a respondent registered as a Democrat or Republican. However, this seemed fraught with difficulties. It is conceivable that a person who registers as a Republican may vote a straight Democratic party ticket in an election. It is conceivable that a person may register as a Republican simply to enable him to vote in the Republican party primary election. Some people switch their party affiliation to vote in the primary election which is more exciting or controversial. Thus, the party affiliation reflected in the list of registered voters might not have reflected either the registrant's political beliefs nor his actual voting behavior. To identify a person as a Democrat or Republican by using the party affiliation he names on his voter registration form did not seem to be very meaningful.

Party affiliation, whether one was a Democrat or Republican, was defined as the party sponsoring the majority of a selected number of candidates for which the respondent intended to vote. This linked the variables, Democrat and Republican, to concrete political behavior, voting. As political candidates are linked to political parties, are chosen within a party framework, and theoretically reflect the ideology of their party, the party affiliation of candidates for which a person plans to vote was seen as meaningful and appropriate.

In obtaining a measure of political affiliation, three major candidate races were selected and an assessment was made of how many Republican candidates and how many Democratic candidates the voter planned to vote for in these three races. A respondent was considered to be a Republican if he said he intended to vote for at last two Republican candiates for the three offices. He was considered to be a Democrat if he said he intended to vote for at least two Democratic candidates for the three offices. There were some methodological problems with this measurement. There was no guarantee that the respondent would in fact vote for the candidates he said he intended to vote for. However, no measurement technique can overcome this problem. Even if a researcher asks a respondent who he voted for after an election, there is no guarantee that the respondent will tell the truth; in fact, there is more likelihood of measurement error after the election, as respondents will be more apt to say they voted for the winner. As our measurements were taken within two weeks of the election, it was felt that the respondent's inclinations to vote for a candidate at the time would probably be reflected in his actual voting behavior.

We will frequently refer to the above-mentioned study to illustrate the stages which are usually used by survey researchers to test hypotheses and evaluate theories. We will focus on how survey research is used to test hypotheses. This research design is particularly conducive to obtaining a significant amount of data from many respondents, which allows one to use statistical analysis in interpreting and giving meaning to data.

As we have stated, the first step in testing a hypothesis is to clearly articulate the meaning of that hypothesis, which requires explicitly defining all concepts within the hypothesis.

Once this is done, empirical indicators (questions you can ask to measure the concepts) can be designed which are consistent with the definition. The construction of a research instrument involves constructing empirical indicators for all concepts in the hypotheses to be tested by the research.

Before a research instrument can be effectively designed, some attention must be given to sampling proceures. The nature of the population to be studied and the way in which samples are drawn from that population can affect the wording of items, the order of items, and the number of items in a research instrument. It is to an examination of sampling, then, that we now turn.

SAMPLING

We mentioned in the previous chapter that basically there are two approaches to sampling: non-probability sampling and probability sampling. In non-probability sampling, one does not assess the chances that members of a population have of being included in the sample. The advantage of this approach is that it is easy and economical in that it requires less control over the sampling procedure. The disadvantage of non-probability sampling is that it eliminates the possibility of making certain statistical inferences about the data obtained. One cannot, for instance, assess the probability that the data obtained is the result of chance factors affecting the characteristics of the sample rather than the result of the independent variables one is examining. In selecting a sample of respondents for our voting behavior study, three non-probability sampling procedures were considered: accidental sampling, quota sampling, and purposive sampling.

The researcher engaged in *accidental sampling* takes people as they happen to walk by and asks them to participate in his research. There is no appraisal of the size of the population from which the sample is drawn. Participants are drawn from whomever walks by when the interviewer is not busy interviewing someone else.

If we were to use accidental sampling in our study of political behavior, we could stand on street corners and seek interviews with people as they walk by or we could ring the doorbell of whatever homes we chose. Both would constitute accidental sampling.

If I sent a class of students out and told each student to interview five registered voters of the county and told them they could obtain their respondents in any way they chose, they would inevitably gather an accidental sample.

Accidental sampling is not to be confused with random sampling; they are not the same thing. Random sampling involves very elaborate sampling procedures which insure a random selection of respondents from a clearly defined, finite population.

Quota sampling involves setting sampling restrictions so that a given percentage of the total sample will contain persons having a particular characteristic. Once this quota is reached, no other persons with this characteristic will be included in the sample. The number of variables that are controlled by the sampling procedure is a function of the researcher's objectives.

In our study of political behavior, we could have sent each interviewer to complete interviews with 5 Democrats and 5 Republicans who were registered as such in the county. This would have given us a total sample having an equal number of Democrats and Republicans. If an interviewer already had his quota of Democrats and, in his search for respondents, he encountered another registered Democrat, he would have to terminate his interview and seek a Republican to fill his quota.

The only control which quota sampling imposes is the absolute number of persons with a given characteristic to be sampled. How these persons are selected is not specified. This is often done by the easiest, least expensive means, accidental sampling. Quota sampling is thus often combined with accidental sampling.

Though quota sampling is thought to control for some of the bias which could arise in accidental sampling, it is fraught with bias also. In most studies where quota sampling is used, the researcher chooses a disproportionate number of respondents who are like himself in respect to critical variables.

Purposive sampling involves deliberately selecting specific individuals who will be included in one's sample. At times this approach takes on the quality of the old informant sampling, used by anthropologists. Anthropologists will frequently seek out specific individuals who are reputed to be extremely knowledgeable, insightful and articulate and will interview them rather than interviewing the "average" villager.

Sociologists frequently do the same thing. Some sociologists find the concept of random sampling to be irrelevant to their needs. If a researcher asks 1000 "average men on the street" why they act in a particular way—for instance, why they stand for the national anthem or why they avoid sitting next to someone else at a soda fountain counter or in a restroom—he may never get anything more than "I don't know" or "that's just the way things are done." These responses do not help the researcher understand behavioral patterns.

To avoid unnecessary, fruitless interviewing, some sociologists believe that, under some circumstances, it is most economical to dispense with random or probability sampling and go to atypical, insightful, articulate informants for information. After getting ideas, perceptions, and insights from these respondents, the researcher then takes these ideas to other respondents for their reactions. These reactions either confirm or refute the informant's views. The advantage of this sampling procedure is that one can obtain hypotheses to test quickly and at relatively small cost. The hypotheses are formulated by a small number of atypical, nonrepresentative individuals and are then tested through a more conventional sampling procedure.

When they can afford it, professional sociologists generally prefer to use *probability sampling* techniques. The greater rigor and control which goes into probability sampling gives the researcher much greater ability to interpret the meaning of his research results.

Four of the best known probability sampling techniques include simple random sampling, stratified sampling, area sampling, and systematic sampling. The best known probability sampling technique is simple *random sampling*. Whether the units to be sampled are individuals, families, organizations or communities, the principle of random sampling is the same, namely that each unit within a population has an equal chance of being included in the sample.

The technique for obtaining a random sample which is most popularly known involves placing numbers or names on evenly sized pieces of paper and mixing them in a bowl. The names or numbers are then drawn out by a neutral party. This procedure is used in the United States to draft personnel for military service. Recent research has brought the randomness of this technique into question. It is apparently very difficult to mix the paper in a random way.

As a result, tables of random numbers are frequently used to select random samples. Such a table can be found in an appendix toward the end of this book. With it is a description of how a table of random numbers can be used.

Stratified sampling involves segmenting the population into categories or strata. From each strata (religious, racial or ethnic groups, socio-economic groups, occupational groups, etc.) a random sample is taken, the size of the sample from each strata often being determined by the size of that strata in the total population. Stratified sampling is frequently used where a population is heterogeneous. If simple random sampling was used in such a heterogeneous population, it would be possible that some subgroups would be excluded from the sample as a result of chance factors. By separating each subgroup and randomly sampling from each strata, we insure that some unit from each strata will be included in the sample.

Whereas in stratified sampling, populations are composed of strata representing people with given social characteristics, in *area sampling* the population is composed of a set of geographically delimited units. If one is sampling from a narrowly defined geographical area, such as a given city, one can take a random sample of census tracts within that city. A random sample of city blocks could then be drawn from each tract selected. Within each block, a random sample could be drawn constituting a given number of dwelling units. It is possible, through this procedure, to determine the likelihood that any household would be included in the sample.

Systematic sampling involves taking every kth unit from the population after starting the procedure randomly. If we have a list of persons constituting a population, such as a list of registered voters, we would select a systematic sample from this population if we randomly select a number—let us say we randomly draw 35—and then select every 35th person on the list to be included in our sample.

There are some sociologists who argue that this is not a probability sampling technique inasmuch as a listing of units in a population is usually not random, but is systematized, either by alphabet or by address or by some other criterion.

In our study of voting behavior in Berkeley, we used a systematic sampling technique. Lists of voters who were registered as Democrats and Republicans were obtained from Berkeley precincts. People on these lists, therefore, constituted the population for our study. Every 86th person was interviewed, but whether he was defined as a Democrat or Republican was still dependent upon how many Democratic or Republican candidates he intended to vote for, not how he registered.

Inasmuch as it was felt that social factors such as race, religion, social class, age, and sex varied in an irregular and haphazard way on these lists, we accepted our sampling technique as, for all practical purposes, a good approximation of random choice, though we realized that our sampling procedure probably did not give us as good a probability sampling as simple random sampling would have.

SOME GENERAL NOTES ON SAMPLING: Deciding on the sampling technique to be used is only one decision the researcher must make about sampling. Another is the size of the sample he should select. The sample must be large enough to allow the researcher to examine all the variables he wants to introduce into his analysis, yet small enough to be manageable.

When one analyzes the frequency distribution of several variables simultaneously in one table, the sample must be large, otherwise there are not enough respondents represented in the cells of the table and it becomes impossible to make meaningful interpretations of the data. If there are less than ten respondents in several cells of a table, the interpretation of the data becomes tenuous, as a single recording error or sampling error can significantly affect the table's meaning.

We may, for instance, think we have a respectable sample of 50 respondents. In Figure 3.1 we examine the effect of age on political party identification.

We then consider the possibility that age is not so crucial an independent variable as is socio-economic status in determining party

		Age		
		−35	35 & over	Total
Political Party Identification	Dem.	16	9	25
	Rep.	10	15	25

Figure 3.1. Number of Persons Identifying with Democratic and Republican Parties by Age.

identification. We want to compare the effect of age and socio-economic status (SES) to see which is the stronger independent variable. If we divide our respondents into three classes--High, Medium, and Low SES-- we might get tables which look as follows:

	High SES			Medium SES			Low SES	
	-35	35 & +		-35	35 & +		-35	35 & +
Dem.	2	1	Dem.	6	3	Dem.	8	5
Rep.	5	9	Rep.	3	4	Rep.	2	2

Figure 3.2. Number of Persons Identifying with Democratic and Republican Parties by Age and Socio-Economic Status.

Suddenly, when we consider three variables simultaneously, our sample of 50 is not so adequate in allowing freedom for analyzing data meaningfully. One mistake in any of the three tables above could significantly alter percentages and might affect the overall interpretation. We needed more than a sample of 50 to run a meaningful three-variable analysis showing the effects of age and socio-economic status on political party identification. If three variables are to be analyzed simultaneously, as is frequently done in sociology, samples should certainly exceed 50 persons.

On the other hand, each respondent surveyed in a study represents expense to the researcher in both time and money. Researchers have limited resources, and these resources frequently restrict the size of a sample below what one would ideally like to have.

The size of one's sample is determined by one's research goals: what is needed to attain these goals, and what can one afford given his resources?

Once the researcher has defined his sample and constructed his research instrument, he is ready to collect data. If he is doing survey research, this means he administers to respondents his questionnaires or interviews. If he is doing field work, this means he observes and interviews. If he is doing a laboratory experiment, he runs his subects through their experiments, observing and recording data. Once the data is collected, it must be organized into a form which is analyzable. If the researcher is planning to quantitatively analyze his data, the organization of the data frequently requires coding.

CODING: We have previously defined coding as a process by which a concept is broken down operationally into a number of variables. This can be done before or after the research instrument is administered to respondents. If coding is done prior to the administration of the research instrument, the instrument is said to be "pre-coded". Pre-coded questions are forced-choice, closed-ended questions.

When data are to be analyzed quantitatively, it is too unwieldy to construct tables and charts from questionnaires or interview schedules directly. It is too time consuming and difficult to leaf through the pages of a questionnaire or interview schedule and find the question needed, each time one wants to construct a table. It is too complicated to leave all data in the research instrument, because each time one uses the instrument, he must go through a stack of hundreds of questionnaires and must leaf through pages of each instrument to tally answers.

To make data more accessible, it is transferred from the research instruments to IBM cards. Knowledge of IBM cards is helpful in understanding the process of data analysis and the process of coding.

An IBM card has eighty vertical columns running across the card. Each column represents one piece of information which can be punched on the card. The number of columns sets physical restraints on the amount of information which can be placed on a card. This restraint

A simple IBM Card

must be taken into account when one decides which items from a research instrument he will record on an IBM card.

The first three or four columns of the card are usually reserved for an identification number. Each respondent is assigned an identification number and this number is placed on the research instrument containing the raw data (the questionnaire or interview schedule) and on the IBM card to which this data is transferred. This identification system in no way removes a respondent's anonymity. The number punched on the IBM card simply corresponds to the number on the research instrument. The research instrument rarely contains the respondent's name.

The identification of IBM cards and research instruments, by assigning them matching numbers, is very helpful where there seems to be an error in the way a card is punched. If the researcher wishes to check the card with the raw data, he can simply find the research instrument with the matching number and check to see that the card is punched appropriately.

Identification numbers frequently include more information than simple identification. For instance, we can give persons identification numbers in conjunction with signifying their age, race, religion, social class, or some other concept. In assigning the first digit, which will be punched in the first column of the IBM card we can specify that the punch will also signify, for example, a person's age.

Coding Instructions

Column 1   Code 1 if age below 18
                         2 if age 18-20
                         3 if age 21-25
                         4 if age 26-30
                         5 if age 31-35
                         6 if age 36-40
                         7 if over 40

If all identification numbers contain three digits, then all persons having an identification number in the 100's are under age 18, all those in the 200's are age 18-20, all those in the 300's are age 21-25 and so forth. The first column can thus contain two pieces of information, a person's identification number and his age. This is economical. Instead of using a separate column to signify age on the card, we have incorporated age with the identification number freeing one column for some other piece of information.

If an identification number is 325, a 3 would be punched in column 1, a 2 would be punched in column 2, and a 5 would be punched in column 3. Assume that column 4 is used to signify a respondent's sex. A 1 would be punched if the respondent were male, a 2 if the respondent were female, if those were the coding instructions. Each column represents the measurement of some concept. The ten possible alternatives (0-9) within any one column allows the researcher to dimensionalize that concept into as many as 10 separate variables. Usually, the researcher will only code a maximum of nine variables for any concept, leaving "0" to signify "not applicable" or "no response".

The number of "0's" compiled within a given column for all respondents in a sample can be a significant clue to a researcher. If many respondents fail to answer a question or give inappropriate responses to a question, it tells the researcher either that his question has touched a sensitive area, where respondents fear exposing themselves, or it can lead the researcher to suspect the clarity and validity of his question as posed.

What is the procedure whereby IBM cards come to be punched? The data which is recorded on the research intrument (by the respondent himself if it is a questionnaire or by the interviewer if it is an interview schedule) is transferred to a piece of paper called a *code sheet*. A code sheet consists of eighty numbered squares, each square representing a column on an IBM card. A code sheet is reproduced in Figure 3.3.

This frequently involves placing an answer which was written in one context into a completely different analytic context. As an example, we will take the question, "What recreational activities do you most usually engage in?" The respondent will write in answers like sailing, bridge, swimming, going to movies, and so forth. Assume the researcher is interested in whether the recreational activities of a respondent are active or passive activities, that is, the question will be coded in terms of the amount of physical activity which is involved in a respondent's usual recreational activities. He will give instructions for his coders to record a 1 if at least half of the activities mentioned are "active", a 2 if at least half are "passive", and 3 if there is "no response". He will establish concrete criteria for his coders so that they have guidelines by which to code the question. He may list all recreational activities that he can imagine would constitute, for his purposes, active and passive activities. He may define active or passive in terms of physical activity exerted or amount of direct involvement rather than consumption of activity, such as spectator sports. He must establish criteria for coding the answer one

1) 2	9) 3	17) 3	25) 8	33) 3	41) 4	49) 3	57) 5	65) 2	73) 5
2) 3	10) 1	18) 2	26) 7	34) 3	42) 5	50) 2	58) 6	66) 2	74) 1
3) 1	11) 2	19) 2	27) 1	35) 1	43) 2	51) 3	59) 1	67) 1	75) 1
4) 6	12) 2	20) 2	28) 2	36) 1	44) 1	52) 1	60) 1	68) 1	76) 2
5) 7	13) 4	21) 4	29) 2	37) 1	45) 3	53) 1	61) 1	69) 2	77) 2
6) 2	14) 1	22) 1	30) 1	38) 4	46) 1	54) 8	62) 2	70) 3	78) 2
7) 1	15) 1	23) 2	31) 5	39) 1	47) 2	55) 4	63) 2	71) 1	79) 3
8) 1	16) 1	24) 2	32) 2	40) 1	48) 3	56) 3	64) 5	72) 1	80) 2

Figure 3.3. A code sheet. The small number in the upper left-hand corner of each cell signifies the column on the IBM card in which the large number in the cell is to be punched. Number 2 is to be punched in column 1, number 3 is punched in column 2, and so forth. The numbers on the cards are punched on a key punch machine, on which is a keyboard which resembles the keyboard on a typewriter.

way or another such as, stating that a majority of the activities mentioned must be active activities to receive a code of "active".

Coding open ended questions is very subject to validity and reliability error. With regard to validity, the dimension by which the question is coded must be inherent within the question asked. In order to code along the dimension active-passive recreation, the question must ask for information which can be coded along this dimension. The code must be compatible with the information which is given by respondents. One could not ask respondents for the kind of recreational activities in which they most frequently engaged and then code the responses in terms of "engages in recreational activities at least twice a week," "engages in recreational activities at least once a week," "engages in recreational activities less than once a week." The information required for this coding dimension is simply not asked for in the question asked of respondents.

Reliability refers to the consistency of measurement. A measurement is reliable if it measures the same phenomenon consistently over time and if all components of the measure consistently test the phenomenon intended.

Errors of reliability exist when coders are not coding answers in identical ways. If coding is not done consistently by everyone, then the results of the study are meaningless. To insure uniformity in coding, it is crucial to give instructions to coders when all coders are present. That way everyone is getting the same information delivered in the same way. Coders must be carefully trained in their job and part of this training involves watching each coder work for a time to insure that they are all doing their job correctly and are all using the same criteria in coding.

Beyond this, it is important to have coding supervisors present when coding is done. The supervisors are thoroughly familiar with the researcher's objectives and can aid coders when they are unsure of how a response should be coded.

The process of coding is crucial in transferring raw data into an analyzable form. In many ways, coding is a research process which is extremely vulnerable to error. The researcher must be painstakingly precise in this phase of the research process. If the coding of raw data is not done accurately and consistently, efforts made in instrument construction and data collection will be for naught.

Once all code sheets are filled out, they are given to key punch operators. The code sheets will serve as instructions to the key punch operator, who works at a machine which punches holes in IBM cards. The code sheet will tell the key punch operator exactly what number to punch for every column on every card.

Once the cards are made, the punches on the cards are verified to insure that the key punch operator made no errors in punching the cards.

In our study of the political behavior of Berkeley, California rank-and-file voters, we were testing the hypothesis that, among rank-and-file voters, opinions held about controversial political issues would not be related to one's being a Democrat or a Republican. In coding data to test this hypothesis, we could use the first three columns on the IBM cards to identify respondents. In column 4 we could analyze respondents' opinions on the statement, "The government should provide better medical care for older people." We could code 1 if the respondent agreed with the statement, 2 if the respondent disagreed with the statement, 3 if the respondent was undecided about whether he agreed or disagreed with the statement, and 4 if the respondent refused to respond or responded inappropriately.

Coding instructions are given to coders in a code book. There are coding instructions for every column to be punched on an IBM card. On the coding instructions which follow, the number of the column on which the data is to be punched corresponds to the number of the question item. The number in parentheses, to the left of the coding options, is the number of the question as it appeared on the questionnaire or interview schedule. The number of each answer is the code number that would be placed on a code sheet. If, for question 4, the respondent "disagreed", the coder would write 2 in box 4 of the code sheet.

1) Identification number
2) Identification number
3) Identification number
4) The government should provide better medical care for older persons.

      1) Agree

10) 2) Disagree

      3) Undecided or don't know

      4) Refused to respond or responded inappropriately

5) Members of the Communist Party should not be allowed to speak on university and college campuses.

      1) Agree

      2) Disagree

      3) Undecided or don't know

      4) Refused to respond or responded inappropriately

6) Capital punishment should be abolished.

      1) Agree

12) 2) Disagree

      3) Undecided or don't know

4) Refused to respond or responded inappropriately

7) Too much money spent on welfare in this state goes to people who don't really need it.
   1) Agree
13) 2) Disagree
   3) Undecided or don't know
   4) Refused to respond or responded inappropriately

8) Our children would be better off if our schools went back to the three R's - reading, writing, and arithmetic.
   1) Agree
14) 2) Disagree
   3) Undecided or don't know
   4) Refused to respond or responded inappropriately

9) I would favor strong American action to get rid of Castro.
   1) Agree
15) 2) Disagree
   3) Undecided or don't know
   4) Refused to respond or responded inappropriately

10) Political party reference:
16) 1) If plans to vote for at least two Democrats
     2) If plans to vote for at least two Republicans
     3) Undecided
     4) Refused to answer or responded inappropriately

Following these instructions, coders prepare code sheets for the key punchers. When the cards are punched—one card for each respondent interviewed—the data is ready for analysis.

84   Theory and Measurement in Sociology

THE PRESENTATION OF DATA: Once IBM cards are punched, they are processed in one of many kinds of machines or computers that count and sort the cards, according to the instructions given in a program. If one programs a computer to cross tabulate the punches in columns 15 and 16, it will print out a table telling the researcher how many respondents voting for Democratic or Republican candidates agreed or disagreed with the statement about Castro.

The great advantage of IBM cards is that the data is readily available and flexible. The data is easily manipulated on IBM cards. In seconds, we can sort out Democrats from Republicans in our sample, and compare them along any dimension we choose. Such flexibility and efficiency would be impossible if we had to juggle the data by hand.

Once the data is given to the researcher by a machine or computer, he must decide how to structure and interpret this data.

Quantitative data can be structured pictorially in graphs and charts, or in statistical tables.

GRAPHS AND CHARTS—A commonly used graphic instrument that sociologists use to present data is the bar graph or bar diagram. Bar graphs schematically interrelate at least two variables. An example of a bar graph, depicting census figures for the population of the United States at ten year intervals, is given in Figure 3.4.

In reading bar graphs, the first thing to look at is the title of the graph. This signifies what the graph is trying to show. The marginal categories

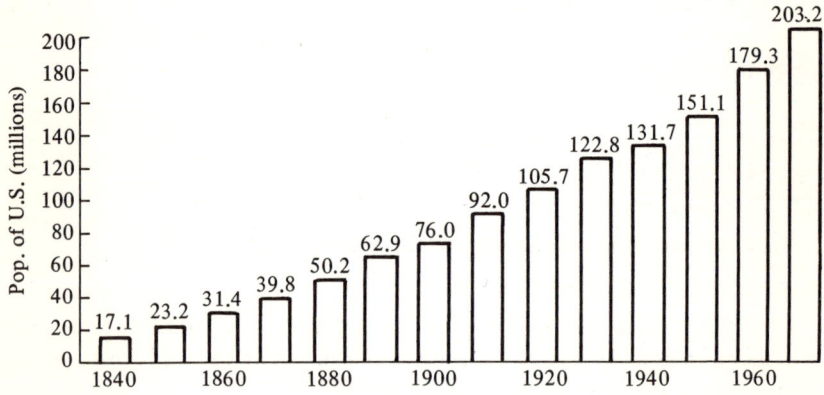

Figure 3.4.   Population of the United States (in millions) by census years.*

should then be examined so that one understands how the graph is organized. Then one looks at general patterns and interrelations. Sociologists do not look at unique events but seek interrelationships and general patterns of behavior. What is important about this graph sociologically is not the population of the United States was 17.1 million people in 1840 and 203.2 million people in 1970. What is important is the observation that population has not increased in a linear progression.

Increase in terms of millions of persons progresses from modest to moderate prior to 1940 and then shows rapidly increasing acceleration in the 1950's and 1960's. Between 1840 and 1850, population increased by 6.1 million people. Between 1930 and 1940 population increased by only 8.9 million people. Between 1950 and 1960 population increased by 28.2 million people and between 1960 and 1970 it rose by 23.9 million. The pattern or trend exhibited by this graph is much more frightening in terms of a devastating population explosion than if the graph showed a linear progression of population. The increase in population during the 1960's was reduced over the increase of the 1950's, which leads to some speculation as to whether the curve will continue to rise drastically in the future or will begin to level off.*

Another way of presenting these same population figures would be on a line graph, as depicted in Figure 3.5. Since census figures are only available every ten years (excluding intervening population estimates), the year the census is taken constitutes the point in time for which a given population figure is applicable. To better depict the pattern or interrelation of these points, the points are connected by a line, hence the term line graph.

A third way of representing the census data we are reviewing would be in the form of a pictograph. Pictographs are often used for presenting data to the non-professional general public. A pictograph is revealed in figure 3.6.

---

* Several factors lead one to be optimistic about a leveling off. Knowledge about contraception is growing. New contraceptive techniques are being researched and developed (although the feverish rate of research development is reduced because public consciousness of drug safety, produced by "the pill" controversy, makes the research and testing of new drugs a very lengthy and costly process for private pharmaceutical firms at a time of tight money). The country is rapidly being more and more urbanized and it is expensive to raise children in a city; urbanization is usually associated with smaller family size. Furthermore, people are aware of the dangers of a population explosion. Population control is a well publicized public issue. Countering these trends is the notion that more people, as produced in the 50's, have the potential of begetting still many more people; we have many more young parents in the 70's than we had in the 50's. Also, with overall economic prosperity many couples may be able to afford more than 2 children.

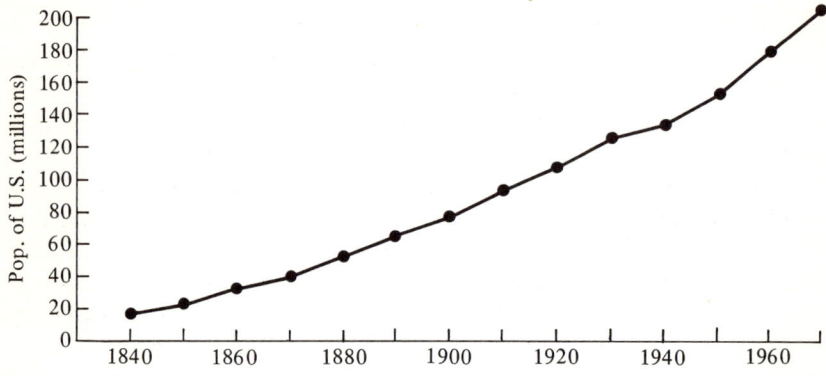

Figure 3.5. Population of the United States (in millions) by census years.*

A kind of bar graph which is frequently used to depict population patterns is a population pyramid. A population pyramid includes information on at least four variables: the country depicted, sex, age, and either actual number of persons or percentage of the total population included in each bar. In population pyramids bars extend out horizontally from the center, rather than extending vertically as in the bar graph in figure 3.4. Three population pyramids for India, Japan, and the United States are shown in Figures 3.7, 3.8, and 3.9.

An examination of the titles of these tables reveals that the horizontal bars reflect the percentage of the total population represented by people of a given age and sex. The reference years (years in which the pyramids were constructed) differ: the Japanese and United States pyramids reflect the status of these countries in 1960, whereas the India pyramid reflects a pattern existent there in 1951.

The pyramids show remarkable overall differences in population patterns. The pyramid of India is very symmetrical with a broad base. This characterizes a society which is having and will continue to have a population explosion. The people who are aged 25-39 are continuing to have many children. This is shown by the long bar representing newly born children, aged 0-4. When their children reach child bearing age, there will probably be many more people available to produce still more children and the pyramid will continue to keep its basic shape.

Evaluating Sociological Theory 87

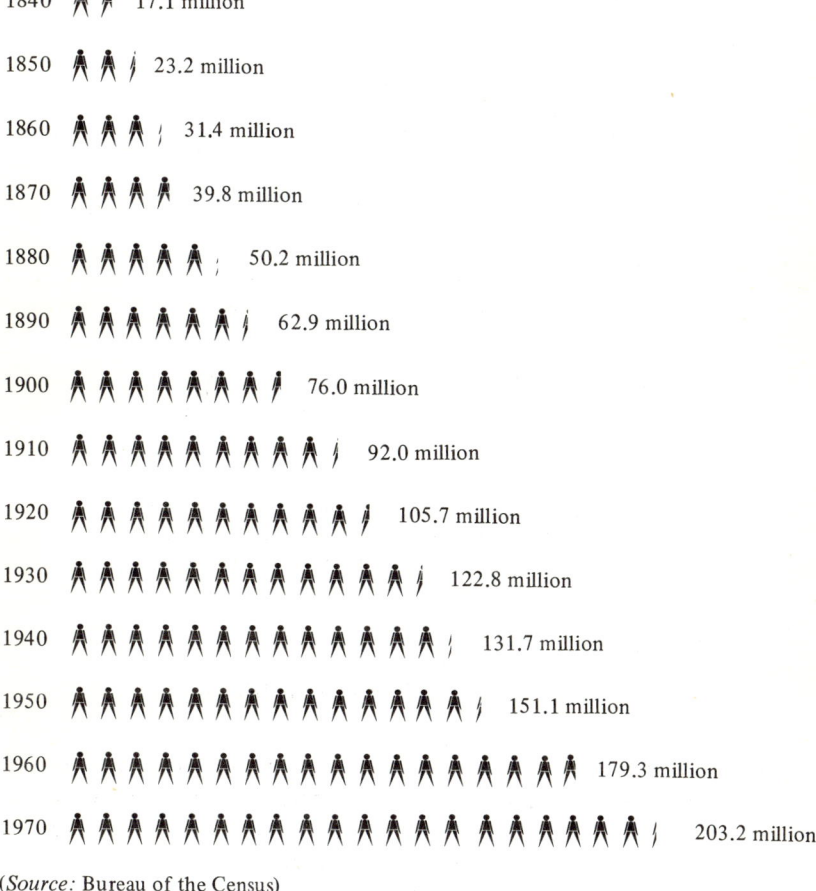

(*Source:* Bureau of the Census)

Figure 3.6. Population of the United States During the Years 1840 to 1960
Each Figure Represents 10,000,000 people.

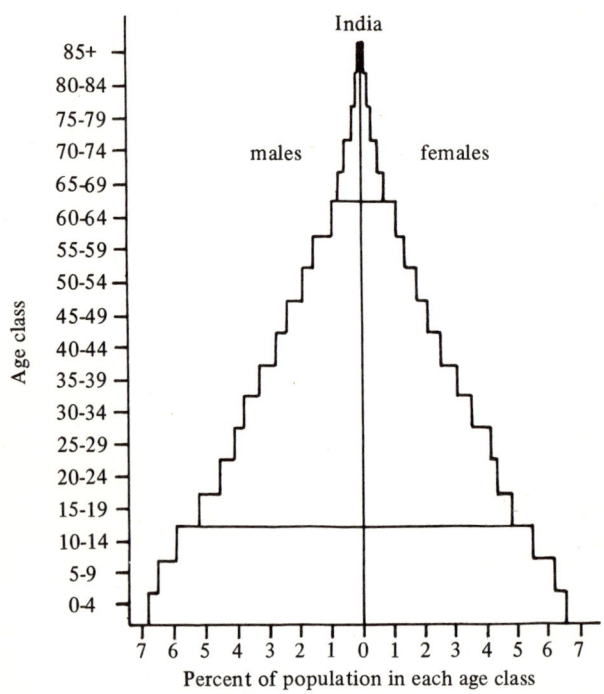

Figure 3.7. Age structure of population of India in 1951.

The pyramid of the United States also has a broad base, but it is not symmetrical. The indentation for people aged 20-29 is a reflection of historical events. People aged 20-29 in 1960 were born in the years 1931-1940, at the height of the depression, when people could not afford children. In times of economic hardship, birthrates drop.

The pyramid of Japan does not have a broad base, but a narrowing base, which indicates it will be significantly reducing its birth rate. This reflects the loss of people, particularly males, as a result of World War II, as well as the legalization of abortion in 1948. The female side of Japan's population pyramid is more symmetrical than the male side

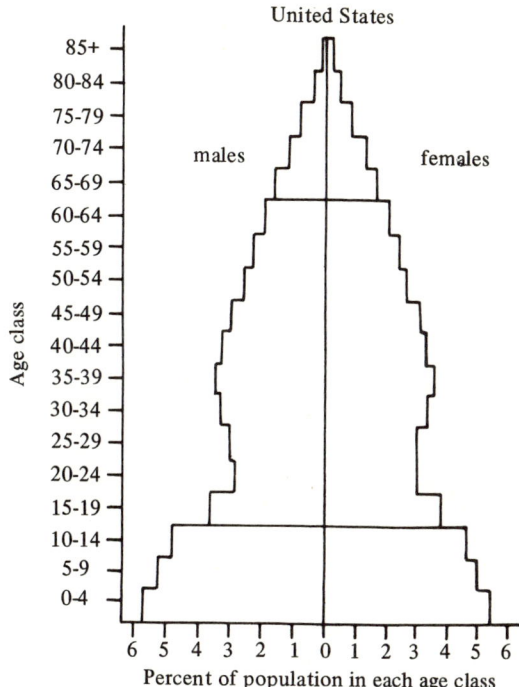

Figure 3.8. Age structure of population of United States in 1960.

mainly as a function of wartime casualties. The irregularity in the graph for men aged 40-50 in 1960 is largely explained by the fact that this "cohort group" was aged 20-30 in 1940-1950, during World War II.

Comparing the tops of the three pyramids we find that among older persons, there are slightly more males than females in India, slightly more females than males in the United States and in Japan.*

---

* Females are said to outlive males in the United States by an average of 6.5 years. This fact in conjunction with our courtship expectations, that the male should be at least as old if not older than the female, leads to severe consequences. Women marrying men their own age or older are inviting several years of widowhood. One reason why our courtship expectations are that men be older, is that women develop socially and intellectually faster than men, so that a girl of 17 may have to date a boy of 19 to find him intellectually and socially mature enough.

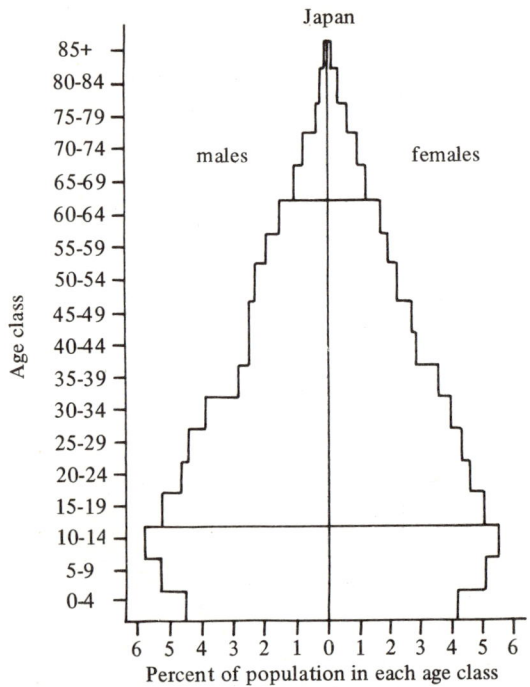

Figure 3.9. Age structure of population of Japan in 1960.

TABLES—Tables are used because they constitute an efficient vehicle for recording information. It would normally take several paragraphs of prose to describe data which can be schematized in a small, concise table.

Tables are not used only by professional sociologists. They are being used more and more in public media to present information to general audiences. Tables are commonly found in newspapers, magazines, books, advertisements, and statistical reports. They are used to report census data, election results, public opinion poll results, test results on consumer products, war casualties, and sports statistics. For everyday living, then, it is important to know how to read and interpret tables.

Figure 3.10 is a *four-fold table*. It is called this because it contains four cells, labeled A, B, C, and D. This four-fold table - arranged with two adjacent vertical cells and two adjacent horizontal cells - is also called a 2 x 2 table.

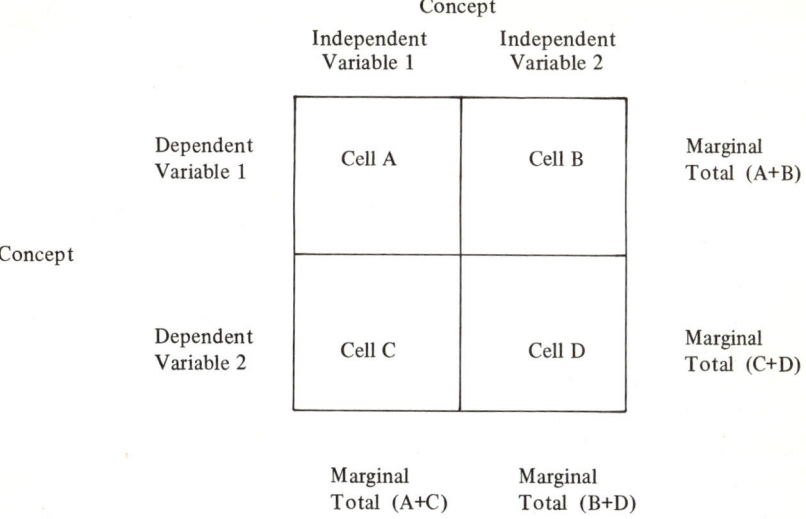

Figure 3.10. A four-fold table.

In examining tables, one of the first things one looks at is the title of the table. This usually tells whether the figures in the cells are "number of respondents" or "percent of respondents". The title also conveys what is being shown in the table. It specifies the concepts being interrelated.

The concepts and variables are named along two axes, a vertical and a horizontal axis. Independent variables are usually placed along the horizontal axis, dependent variables along the vertical axis.

Marginal totals, or marginals, are recorded immediately outside the cells of the table. Marginal $A + B$ is the sum of the frequencies recorded in cells A and B. The marginal totals along the vertical axis will total the same as the marginal totals along the horizontal axis, which is N, the total number of respondents represented in the table.

Marginal total $A + B$ tells us how many persons in our sample exhibit dependent variable 1. The marginal total is unaffected by the interrelation of dependent variable 1 with the independent variables. The marginal $A + B$ is totally unrelated to the independent variables. Likewise marginal total $A + C$ tells us how many respondents in our sample exhibit independent variable 1. This marginal is unaffected by and unrelated to the dependent variables. The interrelation of the

92   *Theory and Measurement in Sociology*

variables, the degree to which one variable affects another, is reflected exclusively within the cells of a table, not in the marginals. This is an important point that we will return to later.

A quality which all tables have is *degrees of freedom*. There are several techniques for interpreting data in tables, which are based on the number of degrees of freedom a table contains. *Based on the marginal totals of a table, the number of degrees of freedom in a table corresponds to the number of cells in which frequencies must be given for the table to be completed.* Figure 3.11 is a 2 x 2 table.

The marginal totals of this table are given. Once we know the frequency of any *one* cell, the frequencies of all other cells become fixed and the table can be completed.

Once the frequency of cell A becomes known, the frequency of cell B becomes known (130) because the sum of the frequencies of cells A and B equals the marginal total of 204. Once the frequency of cell *A* becomes known, the frequency of cell *C* becomes known also (87) because the sum of the frequencies of cells *A* and *C* equals the marginal total of 161. Once the frequency in cell *B* or *C* is fixed, the frequency of cell *D* can be fixed also. Thus this table can be completed when the frequency of any *one* cell becomes known. We thus say that this 2 × 2 table has *one* degree of freedom. In fact all 2 × 2 tables have *one* degree of freedom.

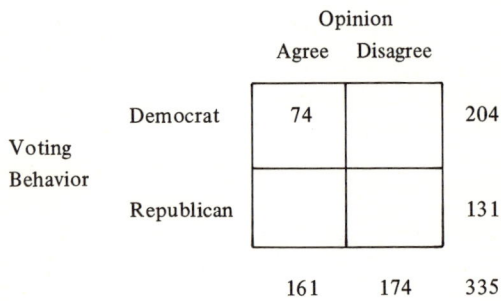

Figure 3.11. Number of respondents voting for Democratic or Republican candidates who agree or disagree with the statement: Members of the Communist Party should not be allowed to speak on university and college campuses.*

	Opinion			
Agree	Disagree	Undecided	Refuse to answer	
				Total 365

Figure 3.12. Number of respondents reacting a given way to the statement: Members of the Communist Party should not be allowed to speak on university and college campuses.

Not all four-fold tables have one degree of freedom, however. Figure 3.12 below is a four-fold table, but not a 2 × 2 table.

If we are given that the frequency of cell A is 161 respondents, the frequencies of the remaining cells are not fixed. The table cannot be completed from knowledge about only one cell. If we are further told that the frequency of cell B is 174 respondents, the remaining cells are still not fixed. Knowledge of the frequencies of cells *A* and *B* tells us that the sum of cells *C* and *D* will be 30 (the frequencies of *A* + *B* subtracted from the marginal total), but we have no way of knowing how these 30 respondents will be distributed within cells *C* and *D*. It is only with further knowledge of either cell *C* or *D* that the table can be completed. If we know that cell *C* represents 25 respondents, then the frequency of cell *D* becomes fixed at 5. In this four-fold table, the frequencies of *three* cells must be known before the table can be completed. Thus this four-fold table has *three* degrees of freedom.

A formula for ascertaining degrees of freedom in a table is:

$$d_f = (\text{Number of columns} - 1)(\text{Number of rows} - 1)$$

This formula can only be used where there are at least two columns and at least two rows in the table.

TESTS OF SIGNIFICANCE: Once a table is constructed, the data within it must be interpreted. One question which can be asked of data *obtained through a probability sample* is: what is the probability that the figures in this table could have been obtained by chance? This question can be answered by administering a test of significance. *A test of significance gives the researcher the probability that his research results could have been obtained by chance.* If there is little likelihood that the figures in the cells could have been obtained by chance, then we infer that the figures are the result of some external factors, such as the interplay of the variables we are examining.

What does the concept of chance mean? In the flip of a fair coin, the likelihood that the coin will land heads is .50. The likelihood that it will land tails is .50. Assume we flip a coin 10 times and in all ten flips the coin lands heads. We begin to question whether the coin is really a fair or a biased coin. We cannot test the balancing of the coin but we can assess the probability that in ten flips of a coin we will get heads 10 times. This probability is $(.5)^{10} = 1/1024$. We are apt to get 10 head tosses in ten flips of a fair coin only once in 1024 series of ten flips.

We must then interpret this probability. If there is not a good probability that by chance a coin would land heads in ten consecutive coin flips, we would infer our result was the result not of chance factors but of some external factor, such as a biased, weighted coin.

How is this discussion of coin flips relevant to sociology? It sets a model for answering sociologically relevant questions of chance. When we seek the probability that a research finding would be obtained by chance, we seek to determine the number of times we would get the identical research results from 100 independent, random samples drawn from our population. This could only be ascertained if we used a probability sampling technique where our population was clearly defined and finite.

The contention that research results are a consequence of chance factors is frequently referred to as a *null hypothesis*. Null hypotheses assert that research results were obtained by chance. The null hypothesis is evaluated by a test of significance. If it appears that there is very little likelihood that the research results could have been obtained by chance, then the null hypothesis is rejected. The researcher must establish a criterion by which he will accept or reject the null hypothesis before running a test of significance. He must say that if the probability that his results could have been obtained by chance exceeds 5 in 100 (.05) or 1 in 100 (.01), then he will accept the null hypothesis. Only when this criterion is established can the level of significance be assessed as supporting or refuting the null hypothesis. In evaluating the null hypothesis, we used .05 probability as the cut off for rejecting the null hypothesis. If the probability that our results could have been obtained by chance exceeds .05, the null hypothesis is accepted.

CHI SQUARE: The most frequently used test of significance in sociology is chi square (X^2). Chi square measures the discrepancy existing in a table between actual, obtained cell frequencies and expected cell frequencies. Expected cell frequencies are the frequencies that would exist in the cells if there was no relation between the concepts along both axes of the table, if the concepts were totally independent and unrelated. The expected frequency is computed using the marginals of a table, which is logical inasmuch as the marginal totals do not interrelate concepts but reflect the frequency of each variable of a concept independently. The expected frequency of a cell, cell A of a four-fold table in our example, can be computed as follows:

$$E_A = \frac{(A+B)(A+C)}{N}$$

In computing the expected frequency of cell A in figure 3.13 we follow the formula as follows:

	Opinion		
	Agree	Disagree	
Dem.	74	130	204
Rep.	87	44	131
	161	174	335

Figure 3.13. Number of respondents voting for Democratic and Republican candidates by whether they agree or disagree with the statement, "Members of the Communist Party should not be allowed to speak on university and college campuses."

$$E_A = \frac{(A+B)(A+C)}{N} = \frac{(204)(161)}{335} = 98.04$$

With a 2 × 2 table having only one degree of freedom, the rest of the expected frequencies can be figured by simple subtraction once one of the expected frequencies is known. The expected frequency of cell B is $E_B = (A+B) - E_A = 204 - 98 = 106$. The expected frequency of cell

96   Theory and Measurement in Sociology

C is $E_C = (A + C) - E_A = 161 - 104 = 63$. The expected frequency of cell D is either $E_D = (B + D) - E_B = 174 - 106$ or $E_D = (C + D) - E_C = 131 - 63$, both of which equal 68.

The formula for computing the value of chi square for any table is:

$$X^2 = \frac{(0_A - E_A)^2}{E_A} + \frac{(0_B - E_B)^2}{E_B} + \cdots \frac{(0_K - E_K)^2}{E_K}$$

In this formula, 0_A signifies the observed, actual frequency of cell A. E_A signifies the expected frequency of cell A. 0_B is the actual frequency of cell B; E_B is the expected frequency of cell B. The value of chi square for each cell is obtained by subtracting the expected frequency of the cell from the observed frequency and squaring this difference. One then divides this by the expected frequency of the cell. The value of chi square for the entire table is obtained by adding together the values of chi square for each cell in the table.

Using the above formula for finding the value of chi square for figure 3.14, we made the following computation:

$$X^2 = \frac{(0_A - E_A)^2}{E_A} + \frac{(0_B - E_B)^2}{E_B} + \frac{(0_C - E_C)^2}{E_C} + \frac{(0_D - E_D)^2}{E_D}$$

$$= \frac{(74 - 98)^2}{98} + \frac{(130 - 106)^2}{106} + \frac{(87 - 63)^2}{63} + \frac{(44 - 68)^2}{68} = 28.91$$

		Opinion		
		Agree	Disagree	
Voting Behavior	Dem.	74 (98)	130 (106)	204
	Rep.	87 (63)	44 (68)	131
		161	174	335

Figure 3.14. Number of respondents voting for Democratic and Republican candidates by whether they agree or disagree with the statement, "Members of the Communist Party should be allowed to speak on university and college campuses." Actual, obtained frequencies are given in each cell above expected frequencies, which are in parentheses.

The value of chi square for figure 3.14 is 28.91. We could also have computed the value of chi square by using another formula, which is applicable *only for 2 × 2 tables*. This formula is:

$$X^2 = \frac{N(AD - BC)^2}{(A + B)(C + D)(A + C)(B + D)}$$

In this formula, the letters signify the actual frequencies obtained for the appropriately lettered cell in the four-fold table. N specifies the number of persons in the total sample. Using this formula to obtain the value of chi square for our table, we make the following computation:

$$X^2 = \frac{335(74 \cdot 44 - 130 \cdot 87)^2}{(204) \cdot (131) \cdot (161) \cdot (174)} = 29.02$$

As one can see, the two differnt formulas for computing the value of chi square yield very nearly equivalent values of chi square but not exactly equivalent values. Using the formula for 2 × 2 tables, the value of chi square for figure 3.13 is 29.02.

Once the value of chi square for a table is obtained, it must then be interpreted. When we compute chi square, we seek to know the probability that the value of chi square obtained could have been obtained by chance, given the number of degrees of freedom in the table. The interpretation of chi square is based upon the degrees of freedom in a table. Figure 3.15 below is used to assess the probability that a given value of chi square could be obtained by chance.

Using figure 3.15, we find that for tables having one degree of freedom, the probability of obtaining a value of chi square of 29.02 by chance is less than 1 in 1000. It is exactly 1 in 1000 when the value of chi square is 10.827. Given our value of chi square, it is very unlikely that the results in our table could have been obtained by chance. We reject the null hypothesis and infer that our results are a function of the interplay of variables we are examining, rather than of chance factors.

We have thus far examined the relation between an individual's voting behavior and his opinion on one controversial political issue. However, in testing our hypothesis, we used six different indices of "opinion held about controversial political issues." Tables reflecting the number of respondents agreeing or disagreeing with these other five issues and voting for Democratic or Republican candidates are given below. For

98   *Theory and Measurement in Sociology*

Figure 3.13 Distribution of χ^2

Probability

df	.99	.98	.95	.90	.80	.70	.50	.30	.20	.10	.05	.02	.01	.001
1	.0³157	.0²628	.00393	.0158	.0642	.148	.455	1.074	1.642	2.706	3.841	5.412	6.635	10.827
2	.0201	.0404	.103	.211	.446	.713	1.386	2.408	3.219	4.605	5.991	7.824	9.210	13.815
3	.115	.185	.352	.584	1.005	1.424	2.366	3.665	4.642	6.251	7.815	9.837	11.341	16.268
4	.297	.429	.711	1.064	1.649	2.195	3.357	4.878	5.989	7.779	9.488	11.668	13.277	18.465
5	.554	.752	1.145	1.610	2.343	3.000	4.351	6.064	7.289	9.236	11.070	13.388	15.086	20.517
6	.872	1.134	1.635	2.204	3.070	3.828	5.348	7.231	8.558	10.645	12.592	15.033	16.812	22.457
7	1.239	1.564	2.167	2.833	3.822	4.671	6.346	8.383	9.803	12.017	14.067	16.622	18.475	24.322
8	1.646	2.032	2.733	3.490	4.594	5.527	7.344	9.524	11.030	13.362	15.507	18.168	20.090	26.125
9	2.088	2.532	3.325	4.168	5.380	6.393	8.343	10.656	12.242	14.684	16.919	19.679	21.666	27.877
10	2.558	3.059	3.940	4.865	6.179	7.267	9.342	11.781	13.442	15.987	18.307	21.161	23.209	29.588
11	3.053	3.609	4.575	5.578	6.989	8.148	10.341	12.899	14.631	17.275	19.675	22.618	24.725	31.264
12	3.571	4.178	5.226	6.304	7.807	9.034	11.340	14.011	15.812	18.549	21.026	24.054	26.217	32.909
13	4.107	4.765	5.892	7.042	8.634	9.926	12.340	15.119	16.985	19.812	22.362	25.472	27.688	34.528
14	4.660	5.368	6.571	7.790	9.467	10.821	13.339	16.222	18.151	21.064	23.685	26.873	29.141	36.123
15	5.229	5.985	7.261	8.547	10.307	11.721	14.339	17.322	19.311	22.307	24.996	28.259	30.578	37.697
16	5.812	6.614	7.962	9.312	11.152	12.624	15.338	18.418	20.465	23.542	26.296	29.033	32.000	39.252
17	6.408	7.255	8.672	10.085	12.002	13.531	16.338	19.511	21.615	24.769	27.587	30.995	33.409	40.790
18	7.015	7.906	9.390	10.865	12.857	14.440	17.338	20.601	22.760	25.989	28.869	32.346	34.805	42.312
19	7.633	8.567	10.117	11.651	13.716	15.352	18.338	21.689	23.900	27.204	30.144	33.687	36.191	43.820
20	8.260	9.237	10.851	12.443	14.578	16.266	19.337	22.775	25.038	28.412	31.410	35.020	37.566	45.315
21	8.897	9.915	11.591	13.240	15.445	17.182	20.337	23.858	26.171	29.615	32.671	36.343	38.932	46.797
22	9.542	10.600	12.338	14.041	16.314	18.101	21.337	24.939	27.301	30.813	33.924	37.659	40.289	48.268
23	10.196	11.293	13.091	14.848	17.187	19.021	22.337	26.018	28.429	32.007	35.172	38.968	41.638	49.728
24	10.856	11.992	13.848	15.659	18.062	19.943	23.337	27.096	29.553	33.196	36.415	40.270	42.980	51.179
25	11.524	12.697	14.611	16.473	18.940	20.867	24.337	28.172	30.675	34.382	37.652	41.566	44.314	52.620
26	12.198	13.409	15.379	17.292	19.820	21.792	25.336	29.246	31.795	35.563	38.885	42.856	45.642	54.052
27	12.879	14.125	16.151	18.114	20.703	22.719	26.336	30.319	32.912	36.741	40.113	44.140	46.963	55.476
28	13.565	14.847	16.928	18.939	21.588	23.647	27.336	31.391	34.027	37.916	41.337	45.419	48.278	56.893
29	14.256	15.574	17.708	19.768	22.475	24.577	28.336	32.461	35.139	39.087	42.557	46.693	49.588	58.302
30	14.953	16.306	18.493	20.599	23.364	25.508	29.336	33.530	36.250	40.256	43.773	47.962	50.892	59.703

For larger values of df, the expression $\sqrt{2\chi^2} - \sqrt{2df} - 1$ may be used as a normal deviate with unit variance, remembering that the possibility for χ^2 corresponds with that of a single tail of the normal curve.

SOURCE: Table I is reprinted from Table IV of R.A. Fisher and F. Yates, *Statistical Tables for Biological, Agricultural and Medical Research* (1948 ed.), published by Oliver & Boyd Ltd., Edinburgh and London, by permission of the authors and publishers.

	Opinion		
	Agree	Disagree	
Dem.	195 (163)	14 (46)	209
Rep.	75 (107)	62 (30)	137
	270	76	346

(Voting Behavior, rows)

Figure 3.16. Number of respondents voting for Democratic or Republican candidates and agreeing or disagreeing with the statement, "The governmant should provide medical care for older people."

$$X^2 = 72.24 \qquad pH_o < .001$$

	Opinion		
	Agree	Disagree	
Dem.	118 (91)	75 (102)	193
Rep.	35 (62)	95 (68)	130
	153	170	323

(Voting Behavior, rows)

Figure 3.17. Number of respondents voting for Democratic or Republican candidates and agreeing or disagreeing with the statement, "Capital Punishment should be abolished."

$$X^2 = 37.62 \qquad pH_o < .001$$

each table, the value of chi square was sufficiently high so that there was less than .05 probability that the results could have been obtained by chance. Under each table, the value of chi square for the table is given, as well as the probability that the results could have been obtained by chance. The abbreviation $pH_o < .001$ is meant to read "the probability (p) of the null hypothesis (H_o), that is, that the results were obtained by chance, is less than $(<)$ .001. Within each cell of these tables, the actual, observed frequencies are given above the expected frequencies of the cells (the expected frequencies being within parentheses).

Once we have ascertained that our results are not likely to be the result of chance factors, we can turn to examine the nature of the relationship or association between variables in our tables.

	Opinion		
	Agree	Disagree	
Dem.	81 (106)	91 (66)	172
Rep.	100 (75)	23 (48)	123
	181	114	295

(Voting Behavior on left side)

Figure 3.18. Number of respondents voting for Democratic or Republican candidates and agreeing or disagreeing with the statement, "Too much of the money spent on welfare in this state goes to people who don't really need it."

$$X^2 = 36.70 \qquad pH_0 < .001$$

	Opinion		
	Agree	Disagree	
Dem.	87 (99)	109 (97)	196
Rep.	77 (65)	53 (65)	130
	164	162	326

(Voting Behavior on left side)

Figure 3.19. Number of respondents voting for Democratic or Republican candidates and agreeing or disagreeing with the statement, "our children would be better off if our schools went back to the three R's—reading, writing, and arithmetic."

$$X^2 = 7.35 \qquad pH_0 < .01$$

MEASURES OF ASSOCIATION: Measuring the association between variables in a table involves assessing the kind of relationship that exists between these variables. There is an association between variables if they co-exist in some regular pattern.

Variables can exist in a positive or negative relation to one another. Variables X and Y exist in a positive relation if they co-exist symmetrically, if when X exists Y also exists, and when X does not exist Y does not either. Variables X and Y exist in a negative relationship if when X exists Y does not, and when X does not exist, Y does.

	Opinion		
	Agree	Disagree	
Dem.	90 (112)	93 (71)	183
Rep.	97 (75)	26 (48)	123
	187	119	

(Voting Behavior on left side)

Figure 3.20. Number of respondents voting for Democratic or Republican candidates and agreeing or disagreeing with the statement, "I would favor strong American action to get rid of Castro."

$$X^2 = 27.66 \qquad pH_0 < .001$$

The hypothesis we are testing states that there is no association between agreeing or disagreeing with controversial political statements and voting for Democratic or Republican candidates. It is possible to measure whether there is or is not an association between the variables mentioned, using the data obtained. If there is an association one can assess whether it is a positive or negative association. It is further possible to measure the strength of the association between our four variables.

We start by examining the concept of zero association. *Zero association* exists when there is absolutely no association, no relationship between variables in a table. Zero association exists when variables have absolutely no effect on one another. When we computed the expected frequencies of cells in figuring the value of chi square, we sought the frequency that would exist in the cell if there was zero association between variables in the table. If the expected frequencies of cells is the same as the actual frequencies in cells of a table, the table exhibits zero association.

Figure 3.21 exhibits zero association between the variables. The values within the cells are actual, obtained frequencies. We can provide evidence that there is zero association between the variables by computing the expected frequencies of the cells. The expected frequency of cell

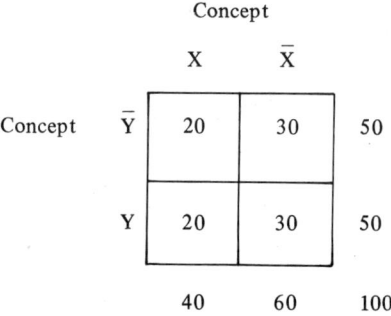

Figure 3.21. Number of persons exhibiting qualities X and Y.

A, the frequency that would exist if there were zero association between the variables is:

$$E_A = \frac{(A + B)(A + C)}{N} = \frac{(50)(40)}{100} = 20$$

This is the same as the actual frequency of cell A and therefore there is no association between variables in the table. Inasmuch as there is only one degree of freedom in this table, we need not compute the expected frequencies of the other cells in the table, as they are fixed, once the expected frequency of cell A is known. The expected frequencies of all cells in the table will equal the actual frequencies.

We have just given one way of perceiving zero association, where actual cell frequencies equal expected cell frequencies.

There is another way of viewing zero association. If there is no association between variables in a table, the ratio of the marginal totals is perfectly duplicated within the cells of the table. The marginal totals, remember, simply reflect the frequency of one variable within a sample. Marginal totals do not reflect the interrelation of variables. The interrelation of variables is only given within the cells of a table. If the ratio of the frequencies within vertically aligned cells of a table mirrors the ratio of the vertically aligned marginals, and if the ratio of the frequencies within horizontally aligned cells of a table mirrors the ratio of the horizontally aligned marginals, then the two variables which are being cross-tabulated have little or no effect on one another; they are relatively independent of one another; there is little or no association between the two variables. In figure 3.21, the ratio of the marginals along the vertical axis is 1:1 (50:50). The ratios of the frequencies in the vertically adjacent cells are also 1:1 (20:20 and 30:30). The ratios of the frequencies within the cells perfectly mirror the ratio of the marginals, connoting zero association.

The ratio of the horizontal marginals is 2:3 (40:60). The ratio of the frequencies in the horizontally adjacent cells is also 2:3 (20:30 and 20:30). The ratios of the frequencies within the cells perfectly mirror the ratio of the marginals. Figure 3.21 reflects zero association between variables.

Having discussed the meaning and diagnosis of zero association, we can now examine association between variables. Association is often used synonymously with the term "correlation." The concept can be understood by means of a correlation matrix.

A correlation matrix plots responses along axes so that one can see the nature of the distribution of responses. If we asked respondents to assess whether they strongly agreed, agreed, were neutral about, disagreed or strongly disagreed with a controversial political statement, such as "capital punishment should be abolished," and if we then asked respondents how many of six Democratic political candidates they intended to vote for, we could construct a correlation matrix and plot responses on this matrix as in Figure 3.22.

Each dot in the matrix represents a respondent. If the dots are arranged in roughly this order, we can see that the more people agree with the statement, the more they will consistently vote for Democratic candidates. We can say that agreeing with the statement and voting for

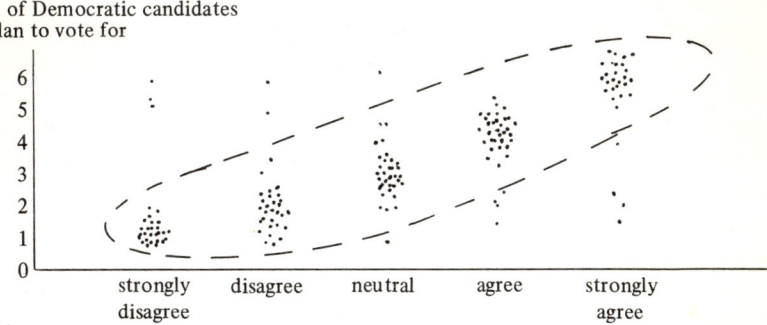

Figure 3.22. Correlation matrix of responses measuring opinion on the statement, "Capital punishment should be abolished" with number of Democratic candidates one plans to vote for.

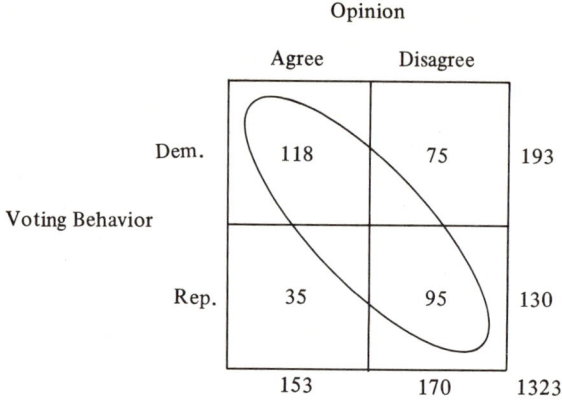

Figure 3.23. Number of respondents voting for Democratic or Republican candidates and agreeing or disagreeing with the statement, "Capital Punishment Should be Abolished."

Democratic candiates are positively related. This is given to us by the direction of the responses, diagonally across the matrix.

We can apply the same visual representation to the study of tables. One can look for the cells with the largest and smallest frequencies within them, and see if the cells with the largest frequencies are diagonally across from one another or not. If they are, then we can visually interpret the table. In figure 3.23, we can see that the largest cell frequencies lie in cells A and D.

Viewed as a correlation matrix, we can see that there seems to be an association between opinion on this issue and voting behavior, such that Democrats will tend to agree with the statement and Republicans will tend to disagree with it.

In figure 3.24, the cells having the largest frequencies are cells B and C, indicating an association between variables such that people who disagree with the statement will tend to vote for Democratic candidates and people who agree with the statement will tend to vote for Republican candidates.

Where there is a strong tendency for responses to be heavily weighted in diagonal cells of a 2 × 2 table, it is easy to interpret the table at a glance. However, the frequencies in many tables are not so definitively arranged that the association between variables can be seen at a glance. In such cases we have to employ measures of association.

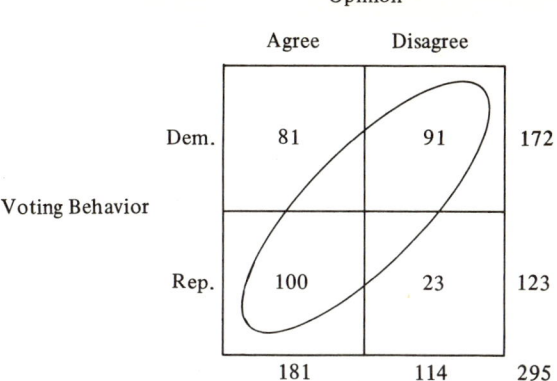

Figure 3.24. Number of respondents voting for Democratic or Republican candidates and agreeing or disagreeing with the statement, "Too much of the money spent on welfare in this state goes to people who don't really need it."

There are several techniques employed by sociologists to measure the level of association between variables. One measure we will discuss here is Yule's Q, which is comparatively simple, relative to other measures, and is used frequently by sociologists.

YULE'S Q: This measure first appeared in a paper published in 1912 and written by the British statistician G. Udny Yule. He named the measure Q in honor of the French statistician Quetelet. Being a measure of association, Q is zero when the two variables studied are independent. The strongest possible positive association between variables is +1.00. The strongest possible negative association between variables is -1.00. When computing Q, the coefficient should be computed to three decimal places and rounded off to two. The formula for computing Yule's Q is:

$$Q = \frac{(B\ C) - (A\ D)}{(B\ C) + (A\ D)}$$

A, B, C, and D signify the actual frequencies in cells A, B, C, and D of a table. This formula has built within it certain assumptions about the way in which the 2 × 2 table is structured. It assumes that tables are arranged in the following configuration:

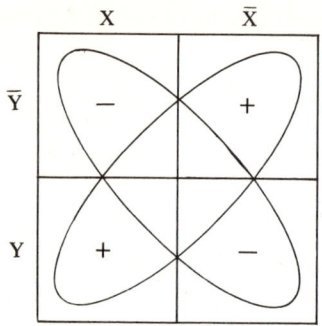

There is a positive association between X and Y if, when X occurs, Y occurs also and when $\bar{X}$ (not X) occurs, $\bar{Y}$ (not Y) occurs also. This means that a positive value of Yules' Q will exist, signifying a positive association between variables X and Y, where the greatest frequency of respondents falls in cells B and C.

A negative association between variables will be found, using the above formula, if the greatest concentration of respondents fall in cells A and D. This negative association exists because, with a table established in the above format, in the majority of cases where X occurs, $\bar{Y}$ occurs (cell A) and where Y occurs $\bar{X}$ occurs (cell D). This is a negative association by definition.

It should be pointed out that there is nothing sacred about arranging a 2 × 2 table in the above format. Particularly where variables in a 2 × 2 table are arranged in a nominal scale, the order in which the variables exist along an axis is arbitrary. Where nominal scales are used, the structure of the variables along an axis is not nearly as important as the meaning given to these variables.

If one arranges a table as above and the majority of respondents fall in cells A and D, then there is a positive association between variables X

and Y, which can be measured by altering the formula for Yules' Q to be

$$Q = \frac{(A\ D) - (B\ C)}{(A\ D) + (B\ C)}$$

This alteration gives one the same value of Q as did the first formula; this altered formula simply reverses the sign (+ or −) of the value of Q. The formula one uses to obtain the value of Q is based upon clearly establishing the variables which will be designated by X and $\overline{X}$ and Y and $\overline{Y}$ and an awareness of the structure of the table to be interpreted.

We will compute the value of Yules' Q using our first formula and therein signify 'agreeing with the statement' as variable X, 'disagreeing with the statement' as variable $\overline{X}$, 'voting for Democratic candidates' as $\overline{Y}$, and 'voting for Republican candidates' as Y. A positive association between variables X and Y would thus mean that people who agreed with the statement were inclined to vote for Republican candidates and respondents who disagreed with the statement were inclined to vote for Democratic candidates. A negative value of Q would mean that respondents who agreed with the statement were inclined to vote for Democratic candidates and those who disagreed with the statement were inclined to vote for Republican candidates.

We compute the value of Yules' Q as follows:

$$Q = \frac{(B\ C) - (A\ D)}{(B\ C) + (A\ D)} = \frac{(130\ 87) - (74\ 44)}{(130\ 87) + (74\ 44)} = +.55$$

	(X) Agree	($\overline{X}$) Disagree	
($\overline{Y}$) Dem	74	130	217
(Y) Rep	87	44	118
	161	174	335

Figure 3.25. Number of respondents voting for Democratic or Republican candidates and agreeing or disagreeing with the statement, "Members of the Communist Party should not be allowed to speak on university and college campuses."

What is the meaning of a Q of +.55? How can we interpret this figure? Yule's Q is a statement of association. It is a measure telling how strongly two variables are associated and the nature or direction of this association (positive or negative). As a general rule of thumb, we can interpret values of Q in the following terms:[9]

Value of Q	Appropriate interpretation
+ .70 or higher	A very strong positive association
+ .50 to + .69	A substantial positive association
+ .30 to + .49	A moderate positive association
+ .10 to + .29	A low positive association
+ .01 to + .09	A negligible positive association
.00	No association
− .01 to − .09	A negligible negative association
− .10 to − .29	A low negative association
− .30 to − .49	A moderate negative association
− .50 to − .69	A substantial negative association
− .70 to lower	A very strong negative association

Our Q of +.55 reveals a substantial positive association between agreeing with the statement "members of the Communist Party should not be allowed to speak on university and college campuses" and voting for Republican political candidates.

How large does the total sample have to be to use Yule's Q? The answer to this question is dependent upon the ratio of the marginal totals along the axis of the table. Figure 3.26 reveals the sample size needed to use Yule's Q according to the ratio of the marginal totals along the two axes of a 2 × 2 table.

In Figure 3.25, the ratio of the marginal categories for variable X was approximately 50:50 (161 to 174). The ratio of marginal categories for variable Y was about 65:35 (217 to 118). Reading the chart and extrapolating, we would have needed a sample of about 30 persons to run Yule's Q. With our sample size of over 300, the use of Yule's Q as a measure of association is quite acceptable.

Yule's Q can be run with percentages or absolute number of respondents in cells. The procedure for computing Yule's Q is exactly the same, whether there is a percentage or a given number of respondents.

---

[9] From James A. Davis, *Elementary Survey Analysis* (©) 1971, p. 49. Reprinted by permission of Prentice-Hall, Inc., Englewood Cliffs, New Jersey.

	Marginal distribution of X						
	50:50	60:40	70:30	80:20	90:10	95:05	99:01
50:50	20	25	33	50	100	200	1000
60:40	25	31	42	63	125	250	1250
70:30	33	42	56	83	167	333	1670
80:20	50	63	83	125	250	500	2500
90:10	100	125	167	250	500	1000	5000
95:05	200	250	333	500	1000	5000	10000
99:01	1000	1250	1670	2500	5000	10000	50000

(Marginal distribution of Y — row labels at left)

Figure 3.26. Size of sample needed to use Yule's Q by ratio of the marginal totals for two variables.[10]

We computed the value of Yule's Q to assess the strength and direction of the association between voting behavior and opinions held on the remaining five controversial issues.

These values of Q tell us that there is a very strong negative association ($Q = -.84$) between agreeing that "the government should provide medical care for older people" and being inclined to vote for Republican candidates. This means that there is a very strong tendency for people who agree with the statement to be inclined to vote for Democratic candidates. There is a substantial negative association ($Q = -.62$) between agreeing that "capital punishment should be abolished" and being inclined to vote for Republican candidates. This means that there is a strong tendency for people who agree with the statement to be inclined to vote for Democratic candidates. There is a substantial positive association ($Q = +.66$) between agreeing that "too much of the money spent on welfare in this state goes to people who don't really need it" and being inclined to vote for Republican candidates. This means that there is a strong tendency for people who agree with the statement to be inclined to vote for Republican candidates. There is a low positive association ($Q = +.29$) between agreeing that "our children would be better off if our schools went back to the three R's—reading, writing, and arithmetic" and being inclined to vote for Republican candidates. There is a slight tendency for people who agree with the statement to be inclined to vote for Republican candidates. There is a substantial positive association ($Q = +.58$) between agreeing that "I would favor strong American action to get rid of Castro" and being inclined to vote for Republican candidates. There is a strong tendency for people who

110 Theory and Measurement in Sociology

agree with the statement to be inclined to vote for Republican candidates.*

In every case, our data fails to support the hypothesis that there is no relation between opinions held by rank and file voters about controversial political issues and the voting for Democratic or Republican political candidates. It would appear from our data that there is an association between political ideology and voting behavior.

USING PERCENTAGES: Thus far all our data has been presented in tables where cell frequencies represent a total number of respondents. However, cell frequencies are often presented as percentages of a sample, and thus we must also familiarize ourselves with how percentages are used in tables. We can convert one of our tables from representing number of respondents to percentage of respondents as shown in Figure 3.27:

When figuring percentages, the percents always run in the direction of the dependent variable. If the dependent variable runs along the verticle axis, the percentages are run vertically, as was done above. When percentages are run in tables, the number of respondents representing 100% is usually recorded in parentheses below the 100% as is done in Figure 3.27.

	Agree	Disagree				Agree	Disagree
Dem	74	130	204		Dem	46	75
				=			
Rep	87	44	131		Rep	54	25
	161	174	335			100%	100%
						(161)	(174)

Figure 3.27. Number of respondents voting for Democratic or Republican candidates by whether they agree or disagree with the statement "Members of the Communist Party should not be allowed to speak on university and college campuses," converted to a table showing percent of respondents voting for Democratic and Republican candidates by whether they agree or disagree with the statement "Members of the Communist Party should not be allowed to speak on university and college campuses."

---

* These values of Q can be checked by using the data presented in the tables on pages 129, 130, 131.

Figure 3.27 tells us that 54% of those 161 persons agreeing with the statement are inclined to vote for Republican candidates and 75% of those 174 persons disagreeing with the statement are inclined to vote for Democratic candidates. Note that just as the highest frequencies in the first table were in cells B and C, so the highest percentages in the second table fall in those cells.

We can compute the value of Yule's Q using our percentages as follows:

$$Q = \frac{(B\ C) - (A\ D)}{(B\ C) + (A\ D)} = \frac{(54 \times 75) - (46 \times 25)}{(54\ 75) + (46\ 25)} = +.55$$

This is exactly the value of Yule's Q we obtained for this table when we computed Yule's Q using "number of respondents" in each cell. This illustrates the way that Yule's Q can be obtained by using either "number of respondents" or "percentage of respondents" in the cells of a table.

Another measure of association we can use with 2×2 tables containing percentages is percentage difference (symbolized by "e"). The percentage difference is the difference between adjacent cells running in the direction of the independent variable. The percentage difference of the above table is 29 (54-25 or 75-46). The higher the percentage dfference in a 2×2 table, the greater is the association between the variables in the table. Percentage difference is a quick and convenient way of assessing level of association and is particularly useful when comparing levels of association between two or more tables. It is often used in interpreting tables when test factors are introduced.

TEST FACTORS: We have thus far studied the extent to which our hypothesis is empirically validated. Yet we know little about the dynamic process which operates to link ideological opinions on issues to voting behavior. There are many questions still unanswered.

Do respondents' opinions on controversial issues causally account for their voting for Democratic or Republican candidates, or do other factors also affect this voting behavior? Do factors such as social class, race, religion, or sex, affect voting behavior and do they have a greater or lesser effect on voting than opinions held on key issues? Does the relationship between opinions held on controversial issues and voting, hold equally for various sub-elements of our sample or is this association greater among some sub-groups than among others?

112   *Theory and Measurement in Sociology*

In an attempt to answer these questions, we will introduce test factors. Test factors are additional independent variables. We will impose test factors on our original tables to see whether these test factors alter the original relationship between our independent and dependent variables. If they alter the relationship, we will examine how that relationship is altered. The nature of the alteration allows us to interpret the nature of the interplay occurring between the variables examined.

We will introduce the test factor "social class" to our original tables. In constructing an index of social class, we combined level of education

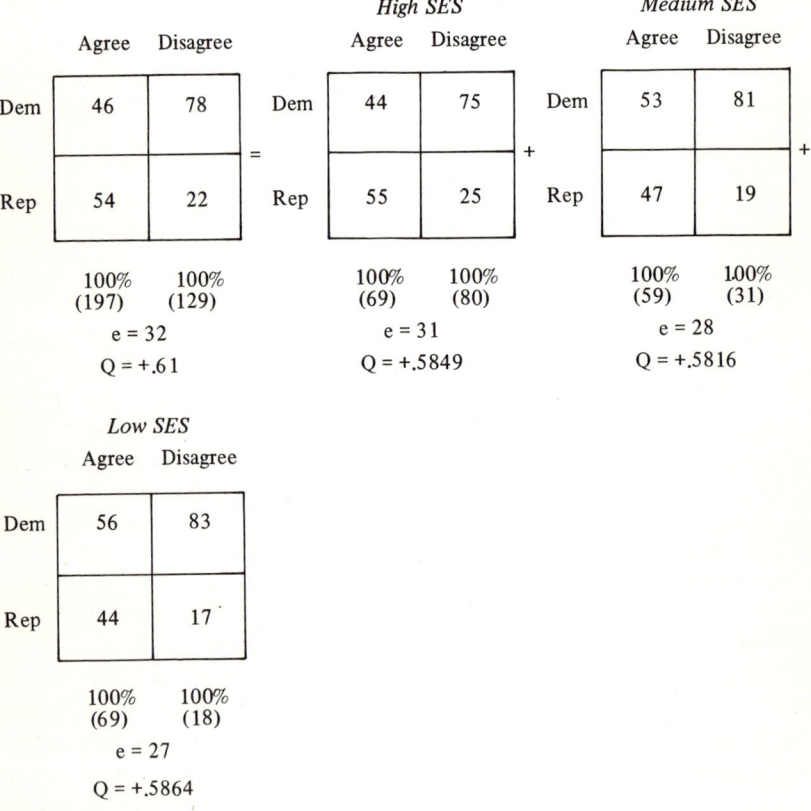

Figure 3.28. Percent of voters agreeing or disagreeing with the statement "I would favor strong American action to get rid of Castro" and who voice support for Democratic or Republican candidates, by social class.

and level of occupation, using the procedure described in Chapter 1. We dichotomized level of education into high and low levels and dichotomized level of occupation into high and low levels. Any respondent scoring high in both education and occupation we classified as having high socio-economic status (SES). Respondents scoring high in one index but low in the other, in any combination, were designated as having medium socio-economic status. Respondents scoring low in both education and occupation were designated as having low socio-economic status.

To assess whether there is consistency between opinions held on controversial issues and voting behavior among respondents in all social classes represented in our sample, we converted one of our original tables into three tables as shown in Figure 3.28.

The first table is our original table which indicated the percentage of respondents in our total sample who agreed or disagreed with the statement, "I would favor strong American action to get rid of Castro," and who voted for Democratic or Republican candidates. This table included respondents representing all social classes in our sample. When we divide our total sample into three sub-samples, based on social class, we develop three separate tables. Each of the three tables with test factors constitutes part of the original table and thus they are called *partial tables* or partials.

In Chapter 1 we discussed the way hypotheses can exist at different levels of abstraction; the more variables there are in the "if ... " clause of the hypothesis, the lower is that hypothesis' level of abstraction. In constructing three partial tables from our original table, we test hypotheses at two levels of abstraction:

I. Opinions held about controversial political issues will have no relation to voting for Democratic or Republican candidates.
  A. Opinions held on the issue "I would favor strong American action to get rid of Castro" will have no relation to voting for Democratic or Republican candidates.
    1. Opinions held by people having high socio-economic status on the issue "I would favor strong American action to get rid of Castro" will have no relation to voting for Democratic or Republican candidates.
    2. Opinions held by people having medium socio-economic status on the issue "I would favor strong American action to get rid of Castro" will have no relation to voting for Democratic or Republican candidates.

3. Opinions held by people having low socio-economic status on the issue "I would favor strong American action to get rid of Castro" will have no relation to voting for Democratic or Republican candidates.
B. Opinions held on the issue "Capital punishment should be abolished" will have no relation to voting for Democratic or Republican candidates.
 1. Opinions held by people having high socio-economic status on the issue "Capital punishment should be abolished" will have no relation to voting for Democratic or Republican candidates.

⋮

The original table tests the hypothesis at level A. The three partial tables test hypotheses A-1, A-2, and A-3 respectively. Hypotheses A-1, A-2, and A-3 are sub-elements of hypothesis A: with A-1, A-2, and A-3 being mutually exhaustive, together they constitute hypothesis A. That is why the sum of the three partials equals the original table.

How are partial tables interpreted? One of three basic statistical phenomena can occur when an original table is broken down into partial tables:

1) The direction and strengh of the relationship between variables in the original table can be mirrored in each of the partials, that is, each of the partials maintains very nearly the same percentage difference or value and sign of Yules' Q despite the test factor. This is called *replication*, inasmuch as each of the partials replicates the original table. If this happens, we assume the test factor has no effect on the original variables. Their relationship is unaltered by the test factor. We assume then, that our original independent variable has a much stronger effect on the dependent variable than does the test factor. If every test factor used results in a replication, it is inferred that the original independent variable was causally related to the dependent variable, pending further evidence to the contrary.

2) The relationship between variables in the original table can be wiped out, eliminated in the partials. The partials can exhibit zero or near zero association between variables, while the original table exhibited a much stronger level of association. When the level of association is eliminated by the introduction of test factors, the analyst must determine the time ordering of the test factor vis-a-vis the original independent

variable. If the test factor *precedes* the original independent variable in time, if it occurred before the original independent variable, then the pattern existent in the partials is called *explanation*. What appeared to be a causal relationship between our original independent and dependent variables was, in fact, a spurious (false) relationship, inasmuch as the test factor was able to "explain away" (eliminate) that original relationship. Our original independent variable was not the cause of the dependent variable - more likely the test factor was - if explanation occurs.

If the partials exhibit zero or near zero association when the original table exhibited a stronger association between variables, and if the test factor is thought to have occurred in time between the existence of the independent and dependent variables (after the independent variable), this pattern in the partials is called *interpretation*. Where interpretation occurs, the test factors act as intervening variables in the partial tables, to destroy the relationship between the original independent and dependent variables. Where this occurs, we infer that our original independent variable was not the cause of the dependent variable. Statistically, then, there is no difference between interpretation and explanation. Both will elicit the same kind of configuration in the partial tables. The difference between interpretation and explanation lies in the interpretation of the partial tables as to whether the test factor occurrred before or after the original independent variable. Both interpretation and explanation allows us to understand the process which accounts for a relationship between our original variables.

3) If the introduction of test factors alters the original level of association between our independent and dependent variables in the partial tables, we can assess or specify the conditions under which the association between our independent and dependent variables is increased or decreased. If the level of association is significantly altered, either increased or decreased by the introduction of test factors, we can specify how our original relationship is increased or decreased within various sub-elements of our total sample. An alteration of levels of association within the partials results in what is called *specification*.

Knowing that partial tables can either replicate, explain, interpret, or specify the relationship found to exist between variables in an original table, we can return to our data and analyze it.

Examining Figure 3.29, we see very little difference in the level of association between variables in the original table and in the partial tables. This is reflected using both percentage differences and the values of Yules' Q as measures of association. A variation in the percentage difference of 5 or a variance of .03 in values of Yules' Q is minimal, and thus we interpret this pattern as replication. The partials certainly do not reflect either interpretation or explanation inasmuch as they exhibit substantially high levels of association—the level of association in the original table is not reduced to zero in the partials. We likewise do not interpret this as specification, inasmuch as the variance between the original table and the partials is so minimal. These tables indicate that opinions held on the issue, "I would favor strong American action to get rid of Castro" are substantially related to voting for Democratic or

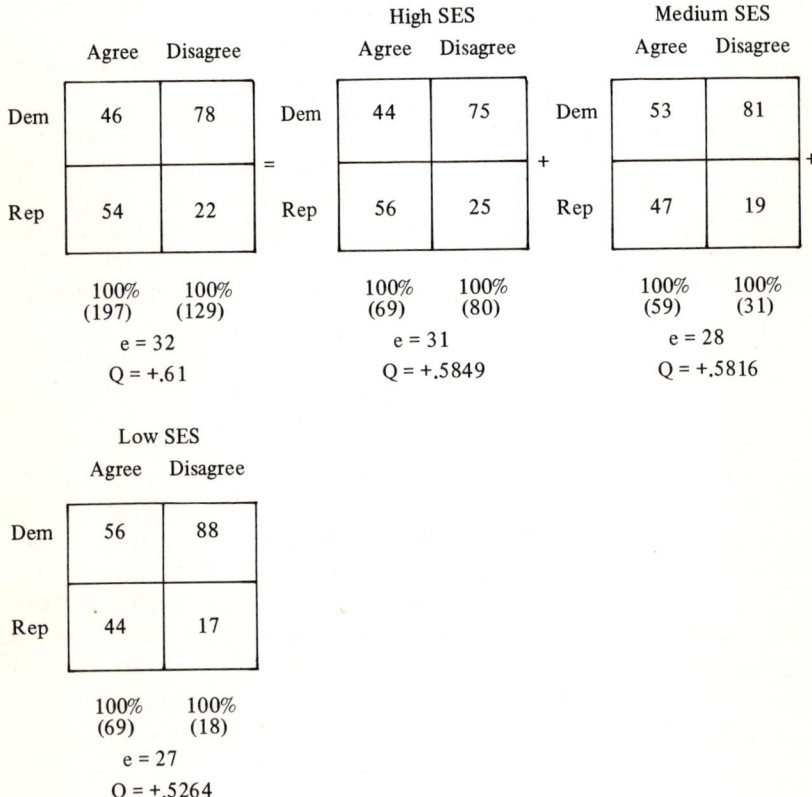

Figure 3.29. Percent of respondents voting for Democratic or Republican candidates by agreeing or disagreeing with the statement, "I would favor strong American action to get rid of Castro" by social class.

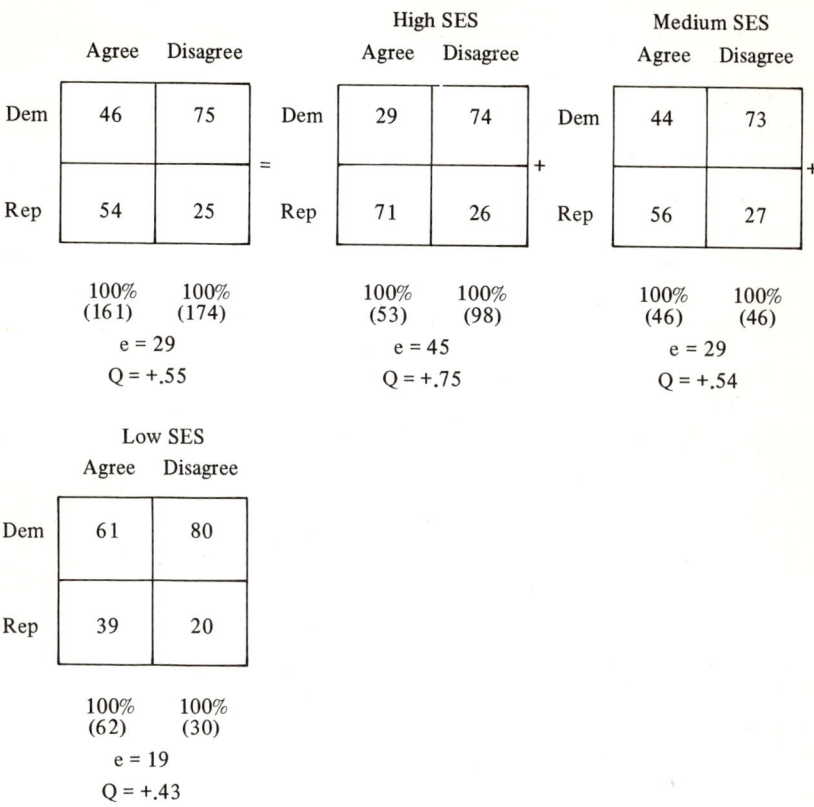

Figure 3.30. Percent of respondents voting for Democratic and Republicaan candidates by agreeing or disagreeing with the statement, "members of the Communist Party should not be allowed to speak on university and college campuses," and by social class.

Republican candidates and that this association holds constant in direction and degree across all social classes in our sample.

This is not the case when we examine the partial tables for our original table linking voting behavior to opinions held on the issue, "Members of the Communist Party should not be allowed to speak on university and college campuses." The partial tables do not replicate the original table. Rather they reflect a significant alteration from the original table. This is a nice example of specification. The level of association between ideology and voting behavior is highest among the high socio-economic status sub-sample.

The level of association decreases with decreasing social class status. These tables tell us that voting for Democratic or Republican candidates is associated with opinions held on the issue, "Members of the Communist Party should not be allowed to speak on university and college campuses" and that the level of association is a direct function of social class. The association between voting and opinion is highest in the high socio-economic sub-sample, lower in the medium socio-economic sub-sample, and lowest in the low socio-economic sub-sample.

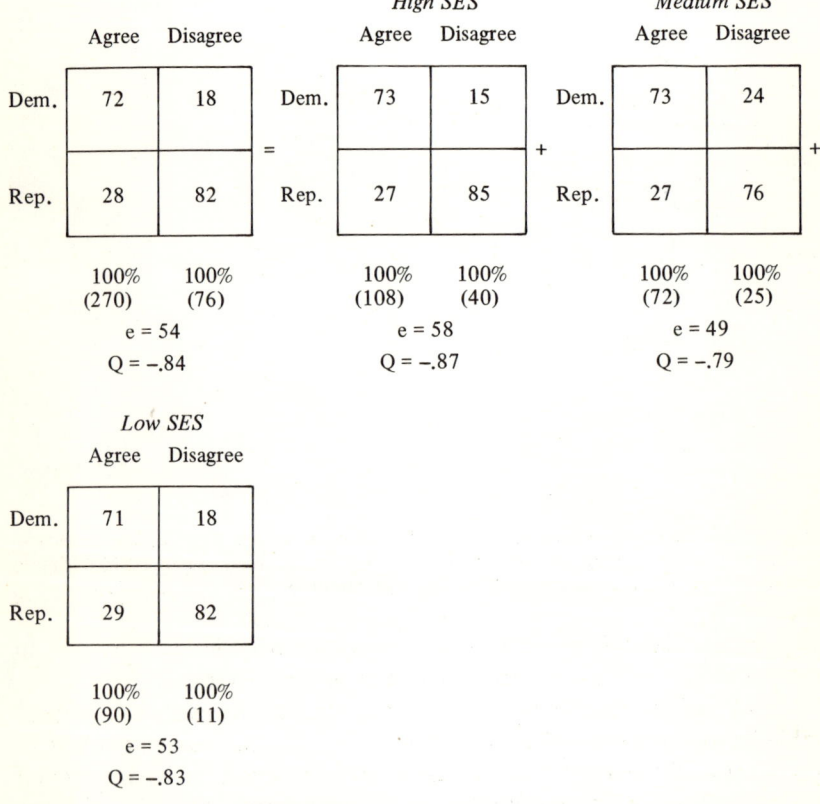

Figure 3.31. Percent of respondents voting for Democratic and Republican candidates by agreeing or disagreeing with the statement, "The government should provide medical care for older people" and by social class.

It is clear from the high negative associations manifest in the partials that neither interpretation nor explanation is evident. The issue is whether or not the partials are different enough from the original table to call this specification. We thought they were. The association between ideology and voting behavior is highest (and higher than in the original table) in the high socio-economic status sub-sample. It is least high in the medium socio-economic status group, but higher in the lower socio-economic status group. The differences in the partials are not very great, however.

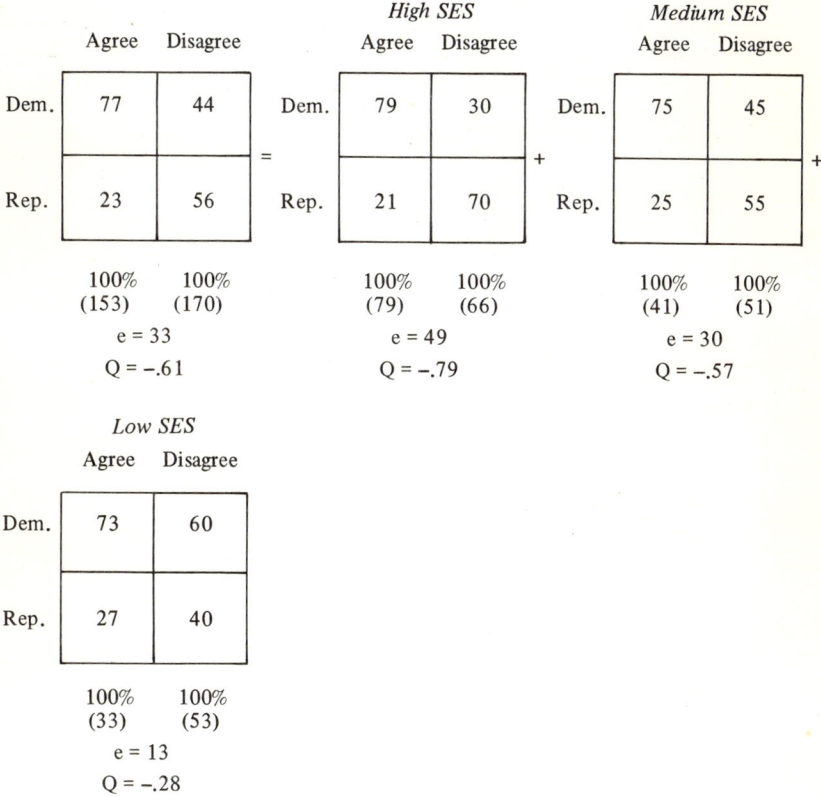

Figure 3.32. Percent of respondents voting for Democratic and Republican candidates by agreeing or disagreeing with the statement, "Capital punishment should be abolished," and by social class.

120   Theory and Measurement in Sociology

In the above tables we return to another classic example of specification. The negative association between agreeing that capital punishment should be abolished, and voting for Republican candidates, is strongest among the high socio-economic status group (where it is stronger than in the original table), less strong in the medium socio-economic status group, and least strong in the lower socio-economic status group. Social class status very much affects the strength of the association in tables on this issue.

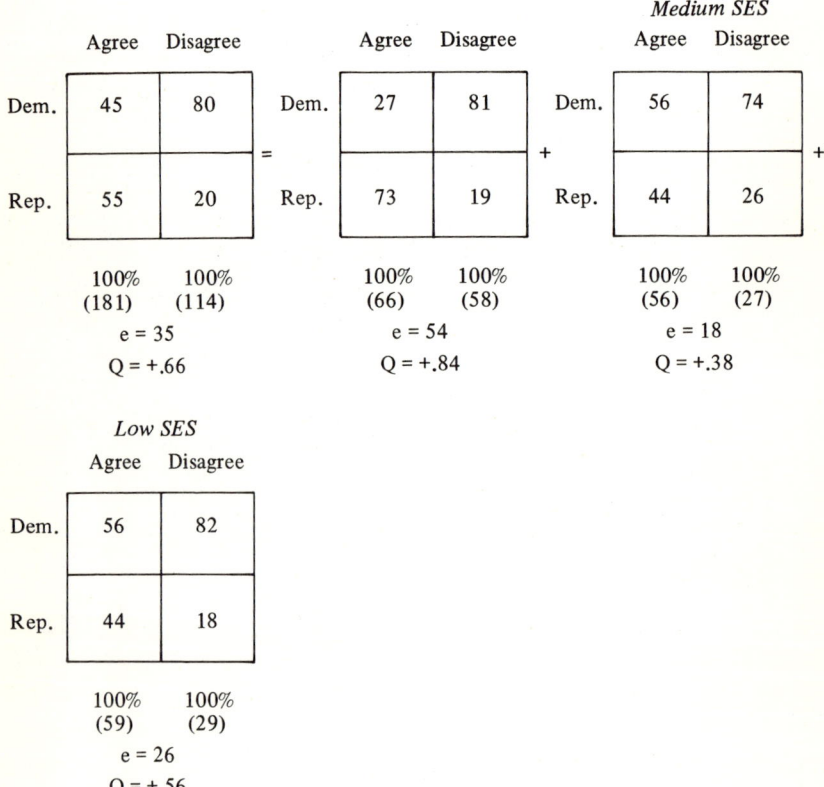

Figure 3.33. Percent of respondents voting for Democratic and Republican candidates by agreeing or disagreeing with the statement, "Too much of the money spent on welfare in this state goes to people who don't really need it," and by social class.

Evaluating Sociological Theory   121

The tables in Figure 3.33 again manifest specification. The level of association between our independent and dependent variables is appreciably altered when social class is introduced. The association is again greatest among the high socio-economic status group (and higher than in the original table), but greater in the low socio-economic status group than in the medium SES group.

In the tables in Figure 3.34 we again find specification, with those in the high SES group exhibiting a much greater association between

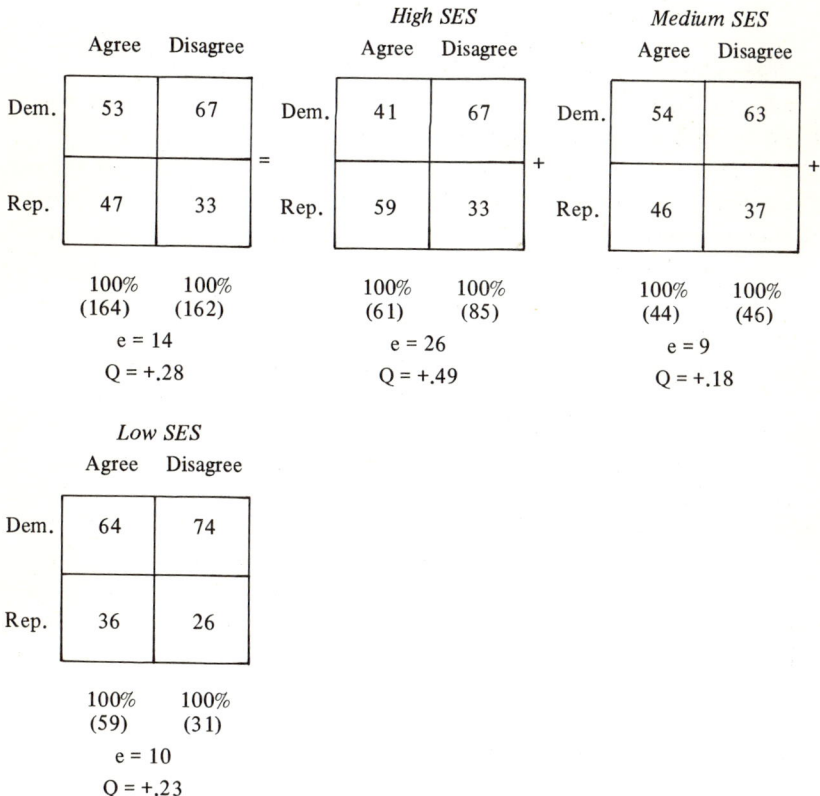

Figure 3.34. Percent of respondents voting for Democratic and Republican candidates by agreeing or disagreeing with the statement, "Our children would be better off if our schools went back to the three R's—reading, writing, and arithmetic," and by social class.

ideology and voting behavior than those of either the medium or low SES groups.

We have found several regularities to be present in the partials for the various issues examined. With one exception, the partials exhibited a pattern of specification, where social class did affect the nature of the relationship between voting behavior and opinions held on controversial issues.

With one exception, the level of association in the partial for the high SES group exceeded the level of association between the independent and dependent variables in the original table. Ideology and voting behavior seem to be linked much more strongly for those with high socio-economic status than for those of the other statuses.

Once we have obtained and interpreted our results, we must couch them in some theoretically relevant context. Our research was conducted to evaluate a hypothesis. By returning to this hypothesis, we can answer the crucial question of theoretical relevance, "So what?" If this question cannot be answered when addressed to a research result, it is devoid of theoretical relevance.

McCloskey found greater ideological cleavage between Democratic and Republican party leaders than he did among the Democratic and Republican party rank-and-file voters. McCloskey left this as a descriptive finding and never systematically tried to account for why the leaders should exhibit this greater ideological cleavage. Was it because, as leaders, they became more aware of their beliefs, or did their beliefs become more crystallized on key controversial issues because of having to set party policy on these issues?

Our data suggests another possibility: that the greater ideological cleavage of the party leaders may be more a function of the fact that the leaders are apt to be overrepresented by people of high socio-economic status and it is by virtue of their class position, not their political leadership per se, that they come to have more crystallized political ideologies.

McCloskey casually addresses himself to this issue when he says: "... the leaders come from the more articulate segments of society, and, on the average, are politically more aware than their followers and are far better informed about issues. For them, political issues and opinions are the everyday currency of party competition, not esoteric matters that suppress understanding."

But he never measures the effects of social class on the ideological cleavage he studies. In specifying dynamics underlying the McCloskey findings, we answer the question "so what?" and make our findings theoretically meaningful. The relationship between political ideology and voting behavior is a function of the social class of rank-and-file voters. Among voters of high socio-economic status, there is great consistency between opinions held on controversial political issues and voting for Democratic and Republican candidates. This consistency declines with decreasing socio-economic status. Our research partially supports and refines McCloskey's earlier findings. There does not tend to be earlier association between political ideology and voting behavior among lower class rank-and-file voters. There is increasingly significant association between ideology and voting behavior with increasing socio-economic status of rank-and-file voters. The fact that "political leaders" have such strong association between ideology and voting behavior may well be a function of their high socio-economic status. Whether "political leaders" are overrepresented by people whom we define as having high socio-economic status is an empirical question which requires research. We only studied "rank-and-file voters," yet this question is raised by our research findings. In this research, we have tested and refined a hypothesis. At some point in time, this hypothesis could be combined with others to create a theory of voting behavior.

A SUMMARY AND A CRITIQUE

The goal of sociology is to create a body of knowledge about human group life. This knowledge is organized in a structured way; it exists in the form of sociological theories.

Theory and measurement in sociology are linked in a single continuous process. Through measurement, through empirical research, theories are created. They must then be empirically validated.

Theories are continuously subject to empirical verification. This verification is done through testing the hypotheses which are component parts of a theory. Because theories are always being evaluated, they are never considered to be absolute fact. Knowledge in sociology is thus always tenuous; it is held to be true until empirical evidence indicates the contrary.

In Chapter 3 we have discussed how theory is evaluated through measurement: theory is evaluated through testing the hypotheses which make up that theory; hypotheses are tested by measuring the concepts within that hypothesis; concepts are measured by using empirical indicators which are derived from definitions of those terms labeling the concept. As definitions of terms are part of the structure of a theory, the rationale for any measurement used to test a hypothesis ultimately is derived from a theoretical structure. Thus theory and measurement are inseparable.

But measurement is used for more than merely testing hypotheses. It allows us to understand and articulate dynamic processes which make normative behavior comprehensible. Through measurement, we can structure the interplay between variables at a given time and place. We can assess whether variables are associated with one another or exist in a causal relationship. We can assess the strength and direction of a relationship between variables. We can assess how the relationship between two variables is affected by a third variable. The use of measurement has immense theoretical relevance, for, through measurement, we can not only describe normative behavior, but account for it. We can come to understand the dynamic processes which bring about regularities in human behavior. This is the purpose of measurement. The results of measurement are ultimately formulated in theoretical statements which are the substance, the essence of sociology.